The Fox, the Bear & the Bunny

SEW PLAYFUL KIDS' CLOTHES

The Fox, the Bear & the Bunny

SEW PLAYFUL KIDS' CLOTHES

Natalie Martin and Naomi Regan

Photography by Kate Whitaker

KYLE BOOKS

Vince and Ivy, Olive and Louis –
our inspiration, our everything x

First published in Great Britain in 2016 by
Kyle Books, an imprint of Kyle Cathie Ltd
192–198 Vauxhall Bridge Road
London SW1V 1DX
general.enquiries@kylebooks.com
www.kylebooks.co.uk

10 9 8 7 6 5 4 3 2 1

ISBN 978 0 85783 367 9

Text © 2016 Natalie Martin and Naomi Regan
Design © 2016 Kyle Books
Photographs © 2016 Kate Whitaker
Illustrations © 2016 Alexandra Ball
Technical Illustrations © 2016 Bess Harding

Project Editor: Tara O'Sullivan
Editorial Assistant: Amberley Lowis
Copy Editor: Helena Caldon
Designer: Laura Woussen
Photographer: Kate Whitaker
Illustrator: Alexandra Ball
Technical Illustrator: Bess Harding
Production: Lisa Pinnell

Please enjoy these projects and make as many as you want for yourself or as gifts for friends and family. The designs are not for commercial use.
A Cataloguing in Publication record for this title is available from the British Library.

Colour reproduction by ALTA London
Printed and bound in China by 1010 International Printing Ltd

Contents

About us

Naomi and I are friends who live near each other with our young families in Devon, England. We met when our two eldest children were small babies and bonded over our love of crafting. We share a special love for designing and making clothes; Naomi is a level-headed, mathematical-genius-type character and I am an inventive spirit with random creative visions that Naomi is tasked with taming. Our two brains combine and together we create the cute type of stuff that you see here in this book.

In 2011 we developed a children's clothing brand that we named Olive & Vince, and this has since become our full-time work. Our dream was to create simple and bold play clothes for kids, with a strong emphasis on comfort and practicality. We felt that there was an abundance of lovely girls' clothing available but the boys got a rough deal. We dreamt of making clothing that could be gender-neutral, bright and fun. Boys in purple and girls in green – it's amazing what's possible if you can just remove that awful tractor appliqué or fussy frill!

We love being really free in how we work. We are completely self-taught in all areas of our sewing, from the design to the making. We suss things out between ourselves and we endeavour to make the processes simple and logical. We've always made our own patterns – coming from the self-taught world, patterns seemed so intimidating, what with their confusing terminology and numbers flying everywhere (fine for Naomi, not so much for me!). So we started from scratch with tables of standard children's measurements and slowly, over many months, began to make our own garments. This is when we realised that I had a flair for designing and Naomi was more than capable when it came to realising the visions into actual shapes and measurements. Between us we have brought nearly 100 unique garment designs to life and we just can't seem to stop.

Both of us have two children – a boy and a girl each – and we know that the clothing that they (and we!) are most passionate about is anything that feeds their imagination. Our families are big fans of the natural world and we can't think of many children who wouldn't want to channel how it feels to be a fox or a bunny! Our fox duffle coat, in particular, has been massively popular worldwide and we felt it would be great to allow crafty parents and friends to get their hands on the patterns and have a go at making them themselves.

For this book we have built a complete wardrobe of outfits with an animal theme for you to enjoy making for your kids (or your grandkids, nieces, nephews, your friends' kids...). Our hope is that we have succeeded in writing a pattern book that you will find highly inspirational, easy to follow and a pleasure to use again and again.

– Nat

WARNING:
THIS BOOK MAY EVOKE ANIMAL-TYPE
BEHAVIOUR IN YOUR CHILDREN.

Guidance

This section covers some of the basic information you'll need while working with this book. As tempting as it is to just start chopping and stitching your glorious fabric, please do read this section first so that you are familiar with some of our methodology.

Level

For your ease of reference we have invented the following key to indicate the difficulty level of each project:

 Beginner

 Intermediate

 Experienced

This book aims to include something for everyone. If you are new to sewing we'd strongly recommend that you start with one of the beginner projects, as these are a great way of building confidence and familiarising yourself with our style of instruction. Projects such as a coat take time and require a bit more experience. There are very clear stages involved in a coat so it's a good project to pick away at over a number of days; but if you try to do it too quickly you can easily get tired and start making mistakes. Don't get disheartened when making any of these projects, you can always unpick a bit of your work to rewind a couple of stages. Aim for perfection and with a bit of patience and plenty of cups of tea you will get there.

Fabric

Within each garment section we have noted what type of fabric we used and which fabrics may be especially suitable for the project. Different fabric weights can affect the finished garment size. If, for instance, you choose to use a thicker than recommended fabric weight, then you may lose some length in bulkier seams and hems. Please bear this in mind when measuring up.

Seam allowance

A 0.75cm seam allowance has been included throughout the book in all projects. If you are using a sewing machine all raw edges will need to be finished with an edging stitch, or a zigzag stitch works just as well. Jersey doesn't fray like other fabrics so there is no need to finish the raw edges when you are using it, but you will need to use a stretch stitch to allow the fabric to stretch without the seams popping.

Cutting layout diagrams

At the start of each project you will see a cutting layout diagram, please note that this is just for guidance on how the pattern pieces need to be cut in relation to the fold and grain of the fabric. You may actually find it more economical to place the pattern pieces differently. The fabric requirement has been over-estimated in case you are purchasing fabric especially for the project rather than using something you already have.

Tracing pattern pieces

When tracing out pattern pieces you can use baking parchment, tracing paper or any translucent paper. Alternatively, you can buy proper dressmaking pattern paper, which is available from most sewing stores.

Marking fabric

Dressmaking chalk/pencil is best for making any markings on your pattern pieces, however if the markings are on the edge of the garment then you can use scissors to make tiny snips into the fabric instead.

Right or wrong side?

It's simple, the right side is the side that you want to see on the outside of the garment, which has often been printed on. The wrong side is the unprinted side of the fabric, which you want hidden away inside your garment.

Techniques

Below are a few of the techniques you may need to familiarise yourself with for the projects in this book. We will refer to some of these directly within the instructions so you may like to put a marker in this section so that you can find it easily while working on a garment.

Working with appliqué

You may prefer to draw out the tiny appliqué shapes directly onto your fabric rather than attempting to pin fiddly shapes cut out of paper. When attaching appliqué it's best to use a zigzag stitch set at 0.8cm length and 0.3cm width, but you can play around on a spare remnant of fabric before actually getting stuck in to find what works for you. When stitching around small shapes, be sure to take it slowly and make continual adjustments by regularly lifting the foot and turning the fabric piece in very slight increments.

If you are appliquéing with leatherette you do not need to use a zigzag stitch (unless you want to for aesthetic reasons) because leatherette will not fray; a standard straight stitch is fine.

Reinforcing

There are some key areas within garments that need to absorb a lot of movement, such as the crotch and underarms. It's a good idea to reinforce these zones for added durability. Coats need to be especially hardwearing and it is worth spending time reinforcing your seams by simply running extra lines of stitching very close to the original stitch lines.

Working with curves

When stitching around a tight curved edge it is common dressmaking practice to snip small triangles out of the seam allowance, in order to allow the curve to sit flat without too much bulk. It's a personal choice, and if you don't want to do this, it's fine to just trim the seam allowance instead.

Attaching buttons

You can do this by hand, but it's super quick and easy to do it on the sewing machine. Remove your machine foot and locate the switch to set the feed dogs to the lowered position. Select a zigzag stitch and set it to the correct width relating to the gap between the holes on your button. Use the presser foot holder (with no foot attached) to hold the button in place and rotate your machine by hand to ensure that the settings are correct and the needle reaches both holes. You can now go ahead and attach your button(s).

Gathering

Some projects require a section of gathering. This is a very straightforward process with a sewing machine. Using a basting stitch (set your machine to its longest

standard stitch setting), run a line of stitching along the edge that you wish to gather, very close to the raw edge (0.5cm is perfect when working with 0.75cm seam allowance). At the start of this line of stitching, stitch back and forth a couple of times as you normally would to secure the end of the stitching in place, but at the end of the basting stitch simply end your sewing without securing and leave about 10cm of thread for both your upper and bobbin threads. To gather, pull on one of these threads whilst gently gathering up the fabric, then secure by tying your threads together. You can then spread your gathering evenly along the length, as desired.

Unpicking

A seam ripper/unpicker is a great little tool for when things don't go quite to plan, such as when you find that you have stitched in the wrong place or you haven't quite caught the fabric. Just carefully pick away to remove the thread from the fabric. You will become good friends with your unpicker! Don't feel disheartened by having to do a bit of unpicking – no matter how much of an experienced machinist you are, it is inevitable.

You will need...

Sewing machine – all of the projects in this book are suitable for making with a sewing machine and need no extra special equipment. However, if you find that you are working with a lot of stretch knit jersey fabrics then you should look into purchasing an overlocker or 'serger' machine. An overlocker produces a special stitch that moves and stretches with the fabric and gives a very professional finish.

Needles – different fabric types require different needles. It's worth having a good stock of different varieties, such as jersey/ball point needles to avoid laddering in jersey fabrics. And don't forget a couple of needles to use for hand stitching.

Threads – always use a nice strong thread for seams – polyester threads are excellent.

Iron and ironing board.

Pins – lots of them!

Tweezers – for those fiddly bits; also very helpful for threading your machine.

Tape measure.

Scissors – a nice big, sharp pair for fabric cutting and a teeny little pair for trimming threads and suchlike.

Dressmaking chalk or pencil.

A chopstick, pencil or similar blunt implement – this is so useful for turning tight shapes, corners or curves right side out.

You'll inevitably gather more bits and bobs as you go along, but in the meantime you will do just fine with this little kit.

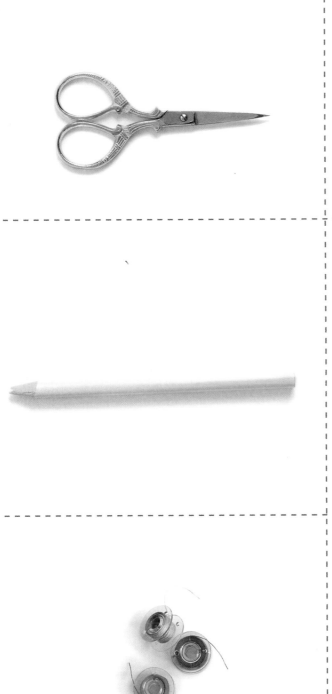
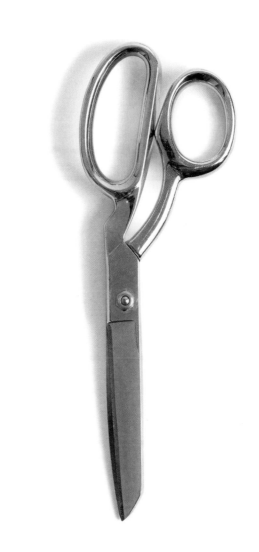

the Bunny

Puffball Shorts

Level:

Cutting and preparation:
20 mins

Sewing and finishing:
1–2 hrs

You will need:
- Pattern pieces A1–A4
- Matching machine threads
- Standard machine needles
- 18mm wide elastic (see sizing guide)

Fabric (all measurements are based on largest size):
- 1m width x 70cm length light-to medium-weight fabric

A little bit more fancy-pants than we'd usually go for, but we can't entirely deny a little lady's right to a pleat or two. With the puffball shape and pink colour palette we've really indulged our inner princess here.

Finished garment size guide
Outer leg length:

12–18 months	23cm
18–24 months	24cm
2–3 years	25cm
3–4 years	26cm
4–5 years	27cm

Finished total waist circumference:

12–18 months	42cm (cut 30cm elastic)
18–24 months	44cm (cut 32cm elastic)
2–3 years	46cm (cut 34cm elastic)
3–4 years	48cm (cut 36cm elastic)
4–5 years	50cm (cut 38cm elastic)

FABRIC: For these shorts we have used a fine cotton corduroy; it is soft enough to be really comfortable and yet strong enough to be hardwearing. They'd also look super cute in a brightly printed baby cord.

Instructions

1 Trace your pattern pieces, making note of any specific markings or instructions. Lay out the pattern pieces on your fabric and cut.

2 Take one of your front pieces (A1) with the corresponding back piece (A2) and attach down the outer leg side seam. You can add a top stitch to the outer leg seams for an extra detail, perhaps in a contrasting and/or thicker thread, but that's totally optional. Next, align the inner leg seams and stitch from the crotch to the bottom of the leg. It's a really good idea to reinforce around the inner leg crotch line by running an extra line of stitching very close to the original seam, as this area can be prone to getting holes.

3 Repeat this entire process with your other two front and back leg pieces.

4 Turn one of your legs right side out and place inside the other leg, right sides facing, with the inner leg

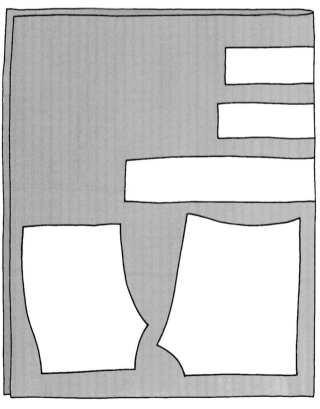

seams aligned. Attach by stitching down from the centre of the top, around the crotch (aligning the seams) and up the other side. Again, you may wish to reinforce the crotch area at this point.

5 Now create the pleats on the front of the shorts. Open out your shorts, right sides out, and fold the fabric of one of the front leg pieces at point B so that point A lies on top of point C, then fold back again from point A to create an overlap in the fabric, and pin in place. Next, fold at point E so that point D meets point F, then fold back again from point D to create another overlap, and pin. Repeat this process, with pleats facing the opposite direction with your other front leg piece.

6 Set your machine to its widest stitch length and run a basting stitch across the top of the front of the shorts to hold the pleats in place.

7 Take your waistband piece (A3) and fold it in half, right sides facing, to align the two shortest edges, then stitch these edges together to create a loop of fabric.

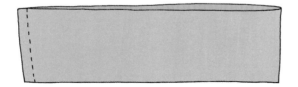

8 Pin the waistband inside the upper edge of the shorts with the top edge of the waistband aligned with the top edge of the shorts, right sides out (right side of the waistband against the wrong side of shorts). Align the seam of the waistband with the back central seam of the shorts and stitch to attach.

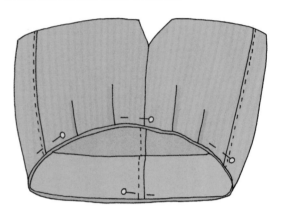

9 Next you need to make the elastic cavity. Pull the waistband out from within the shorts. Press down 1cm of the waistband and then another 3cm to the wrong side, ensuring that the folded edge sits just past the stitch line and that the seam allowance is hidden inside the waistband. Pin the first fold line just past the stitch line here before pressing the second fold line.

10 Remove any pins and open out the waistband. Pin one end of your elastic halfway between the two gather points on one side of the shorts, within the bottom half of the waistband cavity.

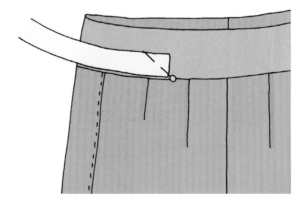

11 Pull the elastic around the back of the shorts and attach the other end of the elastic in the same way between the other two gather points, taking care not to twist the elastic. Run a zigzag stitch back and forth over the ends of the elastic to hold it in place.

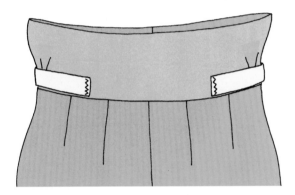

12 Turn the shorts inside out and stitch the waistband closed, pulling the elastic through as you stitch around to allow the fabric to sit flat.

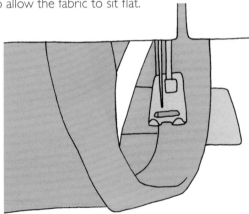

13 Next, fold each leg cuff (A4) in half, right sides facing, to align the shortest edges. Stitch along the shortest edges to create two loops of fabric.

14 Pin one leg cuff inside the bottom edge of one of the leg holes with the bottom edge of the leg cuff aligned with the bottom edge of the leg hole, right sides out (right side of the cuff against the wrong side of the shorts). Align the seam of the cuff with the inner leg seam of the shorts and stitch to attach.

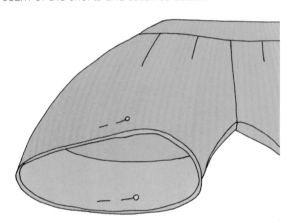

15 Fold and press the leg cuffs up by 1cm and then another 2cm, so that the upper folded edge sits just above the seam line and stitch, ensuring that the seam allowance is hidden inside the leg cuffs.

And that's it – a lovely pair of shorts. There's an adorable little sweater pattern on page 108 that would perfectly complete a totally homemade outfit.

Bunny Duffle Coat

Level:

Cutting and preparation:
1–2 hrs

Sewing and finishing:
8–10 hrs

You will need:
- Pattern pieces B1–B20
- 4 toggles
- 1m cording
- Matching machine threads
- Standard machine needles
- Snap popper fastener tool
- 4 sets of snap popper fastener inserts

Fabric (all measurements are based on largest size):
- 1.5m width x 1.5m length outer main fabric
- 1.5m width x 1.1m length lining fabric
- 1m width x 50cm length outer accent fabric
- 50cm width x 50cm length leatherette
- Optional: a small piece of alternative lining fabric such as cotton, for the pockets and pocket flap lining pieces

Bunnies inspire thoughts of spring time, flowery meadows and a general sense of freedom. This bunny coat is a wonderful symbol of new life, with its big floppy ears and puff tail creating an irresistible urge to hop and bounce.

Before you begin:
This is a big project; you're going to be working with a lot of pattern pieces and fabric, so it's important to be super organised from the start. Try to organise your pieces as the sections of the coat; so put all the hood pieces in a pile, all the lining bits, sleeves, etc. Or, if you prefer, just set them in piles according to fabric type. It's also a good idea to keep the pattern pieces with their corresponding fabric pieces so that when they are referred to by number in the instructions here, you know which piece to grab.

A note on cutting fur and leatherette:
For the leatherette it is easiest to draw the pattern shape onto the back of the leatherette multiple times and then cut to get a really consistent shape. For the fur, place the pattern on the wrong side of the fabric to cut rather than trying to get a clean cut line amongst a deep pile of fur.

Finished garment size guide

Collar to bottom hem length:

1–2 years	37.25cm
2–3 years	40.5cm
3–4 years	43.75cm
4–5 years	47cm

Chest circumference:

1–2 years	68cm
2–3 years	70cm
3–4 years	72cm
4–5 years	74cm

FABRIC: For this coat we have used a synthetic coat-grade felt as the main outer fabric with a short-pile faux fur for the lining and for accent fabric. The pocket lining here was made with plain cotton rather than the thicker fur lining fabric, so that the pockets lie flat. Using a synthetic felt makes this project a touch more complex because you cannot press the fabric (it will melt!), so if you are using a synthetic felt, instead of pressing you will need to top stitch all of your seams. This means there's lots of extra pinning at each stage, and although it looks really lovely, it does take a bit more time. The same applies for the fur lining; it can't be pressed, it's also bulkier and has a bit of a life of its own, so if you plan to follow suit and make your bunny fur-lined, a nice short-pile fur is the best option.

Instructions

1 Trace your pattern pieces, making note of any specific markings or instructions. Sort your pattern pieces into piles according to fabric type, then lay out pieces on your fabric and cut.

2 Begin with the outer body pieces. Pin the bottom diagonal edge of one of your outer front upper panels (B1) to the corresponding diagonal edge of the outer front lower panel (B2) and attach. Top stitch the seam allowance onto the lower front body piece approximately 0.5cm from the seam. Repeat with the other side. Take your outer front centre panels (B3) and attach each one to the front centre raw edge of the main body pieces. Top stitch the seam allowance towards the front centre panels.

3 Place your tail appliqué piece (B4) onto your outer back piece (B5), centrally aligned and 7cm up from the bottom raw edge. Pin securely in place. Use your chosen appliqué stitch (see page 10) and a thread that corresponds with the colour of the tail fabric to carefully stitch around the edge of the tail, taking care not to stitch onto the main fabric to keep the edge neat.

4 Stitch together your front and back outer pieces at the shoulders, right sides facing.

5 Align the curved edge of each outer sleeve (B6) with the curve of the armholes on your outer body piece, right sides facing; pin together, ensuring that the centre of the sleeve lines up with the shoulder seam and stitch to attach.

6 Fold each sleeve in half lengthways, right sides facing, and stitch along the raw edges, continuing down the side of the body and making sure the underarm seams align. The armpit curve is a real danger zone for holes, so it's a good idea to reinforce this area.

7 Lay each of your pocket lining pieces (B7 – lining fabric) onto the pocket outer pieces (B7 – main fabric), right sides facing, and stitch, leaving just the top straight edge open. Trim the excess seam allowance around the curved corners and turn right side out. Repeat with each of the two pocket flaps (B8). Press all the pocket pieces, taking care to pull the fabric slightly towards the lining side, creating a very small border of your outer fabric on the inner side (this will prevent the lining peeping around the edge when top stitching later). Press a 1cm seam inwardly to the wrong side of the fabrics along the top edge of your two main pocket pieces. Stitch across this top edge. Take your pocket flaps and finish the raw edge of both fabrics together with a zigzag or edging stitch, then press 0.75cm to the lining side across this top edge.

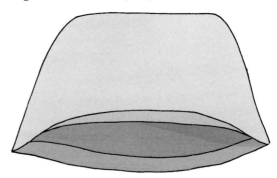

8 With your coat outer body laid right side up, position and pin your two main pockets in place, measuring approximately 7cm up from the bottom straight edge and 11cm in from the front centre raw edge. Top stitch around each pocket and then return to each of the top corners and run a few stitches diagonally across each side for added strength. Pin your two pocket flaps in place with the folded finished edge 0.75cm up from the top of the main pocket, allow it to close over and top stitch across the top straight edge.

9 Next, make the ears and hood. Grab all of your hood and ear pieces (B9–B15), ready to start on the ears first. Before you begin, make sure that you have to hand the thread to match your inner ear accent fabric. Take one of your outer ear pieces (B9) and one inner ear accent fabric piece (B10) and centrally

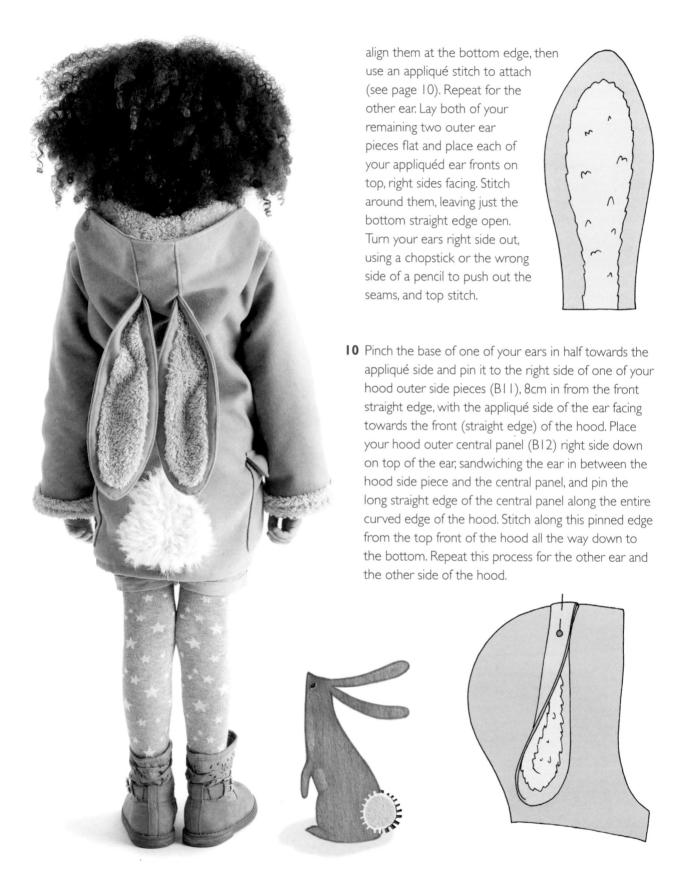

align them at the bottom edge, then use an appliqué stitch to attach (see page 10). Repeat for the other ear. Lay both of your remaining two outer ear pieces flat and place each of your appliquéd ear fronts on top, right sides facing. Stitch around them, leaving just the bottom straight edge open. Turn your ears right side out, using a chopstick or the wrong side of a pencil to push out the seams, and top stitch.

10 Pinch the base of one of your ears in half towards the appliqué side and pin it to the right side of one of your hood outer side pieces (B11), 8cm in from the front straight edge, with the appliqué side of the ear facing towards the front (straight edge) of the hood. Place your hood outer central panel (B12) right side down on top of the ear, sandwiching the ear in between the hood side piece and the central panel, and pin the long straight edge of the central panel along the entire curved edge of the hood. Stitch along this pinned edge from the top front of the hood all the way down to the bottom. Repeat this process for the other ear and the other side of the hood.

11 For the hood lining, lay your hood inner central strip (B13) along the curved edge of one of the hood inner back panels (B14) and as with the outer pieces, pin and stitch. Repeat for the other side so that the centre strip joins the two sides of the hood together. Take your hood inner front panels (B15 – main fabric) and stitch together, right sides facing, along the top short straight edge. Open out and lay the long straight edge, right sides facing, along the entire front edge of the hood lining pieces. Pin and stitch. Place the hood lining into the hood outer, right sides facing, aligning the front edges, and stitch. Turn right sides out, press around the front edge of the hood and top stitch this front edge.

12 Now you're ready to attach the finished hood to the coat outer body. Find the central point of the base of the hood and pin, outer sides facing, to the back centre of the neckline of the coat. Continue to pin around securely and attach.

13 The last job before you can bring together all the components is the lining. Place one of your front inner side panels (B16), right sides facing, against your corresponding front inner middle panel (B17 – main fabric). Pin together along the long curved edge and stitch. Repeat for the other side. Attach the shoulder (top short edge) of each of these to the corresponding shoulder of the inner back piece (B18). Open out your now-attached lining and pin the top curve of the sleeve lining (B19) into the armhole curve, ensuring that the centre of the sleeve sits at the shoulder seam. Attach and repeat for the other side.

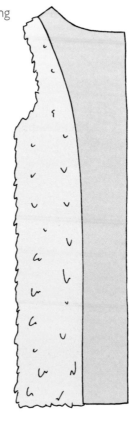

14 Fold each lining sleeve in half lengthways, right sides facing, and stitch along the raw edges, continuing down the side of the body, ensuring that the underarm seams align. As with the outer pieces, it's worth reinforcing this stitch just around the underarm area.

15 If you are going to use popper fasteners in your coat, now is the time to insert them. Lay out your coat outer and use a chalk pencil to mark the positions for your poppers on the front centre panel of the child's left side (right side to look at). Sit the first popper fairly close to the top, so it provides a nice snug seal against the cold, remembering to leave seam allowance. Then position three more poppers at regular intervals down the coat, taking the last popper no lower than the mid-point of the pocket; remember to leave space for a hem plus the leatherette triangles. The poppers for the other side of the coat will go on the lining piece, so be sure to align the top edges of the lining and outer body pieces to transfer your markings across to the child's right side of the lining piece. There is a 4cm difference in length between the lining and outer pieces, so it is important that your poppers line up from the top edge and not the bottom. Now go ahead and insert your popper fasteners. Be warned, making a mistake at this stage is catastrophic, so check and check again that you have correctly aligned your poppers.

16 Pin your lining, right sides facing, to the neckline of the outer body section, taking care to align at the shoulder seams. Stitch around the neck opening in order to sandwich your hood in between these layers. This is probably the trickiest part of this project – just pin plenty, take it slow and you will be just fine.

17 Sometimes you can be left with a bit of a wonky line running across the entire bottom width of your outer and lining body pieces where all the different pieces have joined. If so, take your scissors and tidy it up, but note that the lining is intended to be 4cm shorter than the outer body section so please don't chop this off! Take measurements to compare each side in length so that you aren't left with one side of the coat hanging slightly lower than the other, it's an easy mistake to make and it's so disappointing to discover right at the last moment. Now that you have a lovely straight line to work with, pin together the outer and lining body pieces, right sides facing, along the bottom raw edge and stitch 2cm in from the edge.

18 Take one side of your coat and stitch the front central edge closed, starting from the top. When you reach the bottom, the outer coat will pull around by 2cm towards the lining side; continue to stitch through this overlap whilst pulling the seam allowance downwards so that it will sit inside the hem. Take the other side but don't close this up entirely, leave a large gap for pulling the entire coat right side out. Begin stitching from the top, then part way down leave your gap, then resume stitching, ensuring that you are left with the same 2cm overlap at the bottom as before. Carefully trim the two top corners to remove any bulk from the collar.

19 Reach inside the gap that you have left and begin to turn your garment. Take your chopstick/pencil and push out all the corners. Press your coat, starting at the front seams. On the side that you have left open, take care to fold in the same seam allowance along the gap, retaining a consistent straight edge.

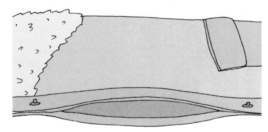

20 When pressing along the bottom hem, reach back inside the lining to make sure the 2cm seam allowance is pushed downwards to sit within the hem and pin this in place. Top stitch a 1cm hem across the entire bottom of the coat, then top stitch the two front edges, closing your turning gap as you go.

21 One of the last details is to produce a little fur cuff on the sleeves so that the lining will peep around to show on the outer fabric side. Push your sleeve lining, right side in, through the outer body sleeve so that your main sleeve is right side out. Fold 1cm of the sleeve lining towards the wrong side and another 2cm towards the wrong side The edge of the outer sleeve should sit fully inside this hem. Repeat for the other sleeve, pin and stitch both sleeve hems.

22 Cut eight 12cm lengths of cording and insert four of them through your chosen toggles. Place to one side. Lay out your coat and pin or mark with chalk where you'd like your toggles to be. For a really good seal down the front of the coat, position the toggles in between the poppers. Affix your toggles to the coat with small reinforced stitches on the child's left side. Attach your remaining loops of cording to the opposite side, making sure they line up with the toggles.

23 Finally, take your 8 leatherette triangular shapes (B20) and use a standard straight stitch to top stitch them over the raw ends of the cording. It helps to disguise the under-stitching if you use a coordinating thread on top whilst keeping the bobbin the same colour as the main body of the coat.

Congratulations on your gorgeous homemade bunny coat, perfect for a crisp spring morning.

the Cat

Furry Gilet

Level:

Cutting and preparation:
15 mins

Sewing and finishing:
1–2 hrs

You will need:
- Pattern pieces C1 & C2
- 2 toggles or buttons
- A small length of cording
- Matching machine threads
- Standard machine needles

Fabric (all measurements are based on largest size):
- 50cm width x 1m length fur outer fabric
- 50cm width x 1m length lining
- Optional: a small piece of leatherette to hide the ends of cording

Formal or casual, there is always a place for a gilet – it is the ultimate style statement. This is quite straightforward compared to a coat, so it's a great confidence-boosting project that'll gently ease you into the world of outer body wear.

A note on cutting fur:
For the most accurate results, place the pattern on the wrong side of the fabric to cut rather than trying to get a clean cut line amongst a deep pile of fur.

Finished garment size guide

Nape to bottom hem length:

1–2 years	29.75cm
2–3 years	31.75cm
3–4 years	33.75cm
4–5 years	35.75cm

Chest circumference:

1–2 years	63cm
2–3 years	65cm
3–4 years	67cm
4–5 years	69cm

FABRIC: The outer fabric of this gilet is a deep-pile faux fur, lined with a floral printed cotton poplin. The instructions here are written with fur in mind, but use your discretion if you prefer a different heavyweight outer fabric. The lining should always be a lighter fabric, such as cotton.

The Fox, the Bear & the Bunny

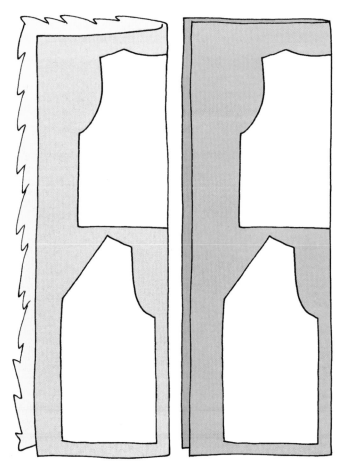

Instructions

1. Trace your pattern pieces, making note of any specific markings or instructions. Lay out the pattern pieces on your fabric and cut.

2. Take your outer front (C1) and back (C2) pieces, right sides facing, and attach down the underarm side seams. Repeat with your lining.

3. The cording and toggles/buttons now need to be attached to the outer fabric of the gilet so that the button or toggle passes through a loop of cording to hold the gilet closed. Cut four small pieces of cording – the exact length will depend on the size of your toggles/buttons. Thread each of your buttons onto a piece of cording. Take your outer body section and pin your two buttons in place (approximately 2cm and 12cm down from the point where the top of the central vertical edge meets the diagonal edge) so that the raw ends of the cording sit at least 3cm in from the front centre edge and your buttons are positioned inwardly onto the garment (the 'wrong' direction for now). Stitch the ends of the cording to hold them in place then turn the cording back on itself to cover the raw ends and stitch over the fold to keep the raw ends hidden. If you prefer, you can appliqué a small piece of leatherette over the ends of your cording, however with a thick-pile fur this is not really necessary.

4. Place your outer section, right sides facing, against the lining and pin along the bottom edge, aligning at the seams. Stitch along this bottom edge. It's always tempting to skip the pinning stage, but for this project it is particularly important because the fur fabric has a different stretch to the cotton poplin and it will want to try its best to come out of alignment!

5. Take your remaining two loops of cording and sandwich the raw ends between your outer and lining fabrics to line up with each of the buttons on the opposite side of the gilet. Pin in place and stitch up the entire vertical edges (centre front). Repeat on the other side, taking care to avoid catching your buttons.

6 Stitch part way up each of the two diagonal front edges, stopping 8cm from the shoulder edge.

7 Next, begin stitching 8cm down from one of the front shoulder edges, around the underarm and up the other side, stopping 8cm below the back shoulder edge. Repeat on the other side.

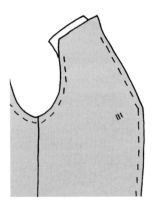

8 Begin stitching 8cm in from one of the back shoulder edges across the neck curve and stop 8cm in from the other shoulder edge.

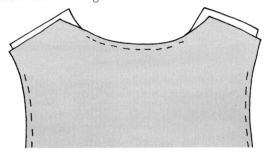

9 Reach into one of the open shoulders and pull the entire garment right side out through the gap. Use a chopstick or the wrong end of a pencil to push out all the seams and corners.

10 Take one side of your gilet, align the front and back straight shoulder edges of the outer fabric and stitch.

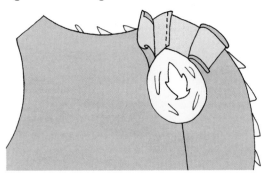

11 The next bit is a little fiddly. On the same side as you've just attached the outer shoulders, twist the shoulder so that the lining fabrics meet, right sides facing, along the shoulder edge, then stitch. The inside of the shoulder seams of the fur and lining will now be facing, hidden inside the garment. Repeat on the other side.

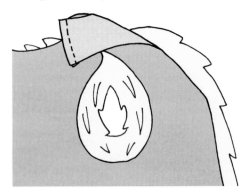

12 Fold over a 0.75cm seam allowance at the open sections of the shoulders and pin at the seams.

13 Starting at the back centre of the neck, begin top stitching 0.5cm in from the edge around the entire outside of the garment on the lining side. Take care to catch the seam allowance of both fabrics around the open shoulder sections and pull the fur away from the needle as you work, to help disguise the stitch line later.

14 Finally, top stitch around the armholes, making sure the fur isn't caught too much within the seams, so that it looks lovely and fluffy.

Give it a shake out and you're all done – one fabulous snuggly gilet.

Kitten Culottes

Level:

Cutting and preparation:
20 mins

Sewing and finishing:
1–2 hrs

You will need:
- Pattern pieces D1–D3
- Matching machine threads
- Standard machine needles
- 35mm wide elastic (see size guide)

Fabric (all measurements are based on largest size):
- 1m x 1m light- to medium-weight fabric

FABRIC: A medium-weight cotton canvas holds the pleats really well, is heavy enough to drape nicely yet light enough to be comfortable. Plain fabrics would show off the shape and design very well, but culottes can carry a bold print brilliantly.

For a single garment, culottes have such endless potential; practical, pretty and funky. We've gone for a knee-length style but it's easy to cut them extra long to achieve a mid-calf length, which looks incredibly cool.

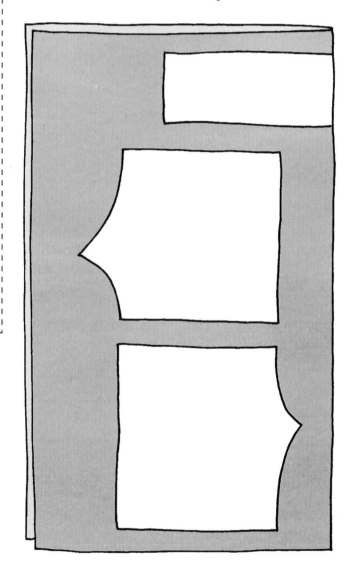

Finished garment size guide

Outer leg length:

12–18 months	32cm
18–24 months	34cm
2–3 years	36cm
3–4 years	40cm
4–5 years	42cm

Back gathering measurement:

12–18 months	36cm
18–24 months	37cm
2–3 years	38cm
3–4 years	39cm
4–5 years	40cm

Finished total waist circumference:

12–18 months	42cm (cut 32cm elastic)
18–24 months	44cm (cut 34cm elastic)
2–3 years	46cm (cut 36cm elastic)
3–4 years	48cm (cut 36cm elastic)
4–5 years	50cm (cut 38cm elastic)

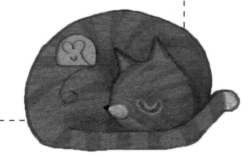

Instructions

1 Trace your pattern pieces, making a note of any specific markings or instructions. Lay out the pattern pieces on your fabric and cut.

2 Begin by creating the pleats on the front of the culottes. Take one of your front pieces (D1) and fold the fabric at point B so that point C lies on top of point A, then fold back again from point C to create an overlap in the fabric and pin in place. Next, fold at point E so that point F meets point D, then fold back again from point F to create another overlap, then pin. Repeat this process with your other front leg piece.

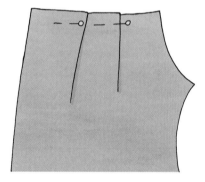

3 Set your machine to its widest stitch length and run a basting stitch across the top of each of your leg pieces to hold the pleats in place.

4 Take your two front pieces, right sides facing, and attach down the front centre seam to the crotch, then repeat for the back pieces (D2). You can reinforce these inner seams with a line of stitching very close to the seam line, if you like, as this area can be prone to holes and tears. Next, gather the top edge of the back pieces to the measurements given in the size guide (see page 10 for help with gathering).

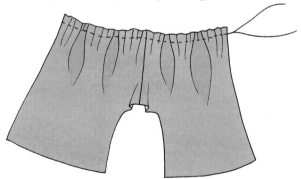

5 Place your front and back pieces, right sides facing, and attach along the outer side seams. Stitch the inner leg closed from the bottom of one leg, around the crotch and down the other leg, aligning the centre seams.

6 Take your waistband piece (D3) and fold in half, right sides facing, to align the two shortest edges, then stitch these edges together to create a loop of fabric.

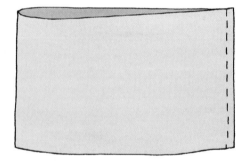

7 Turn your culottes right side out and pin your waistband with the top edge of the waistband aligned with the top edge of the culottes, right sides out (right side of the waistband against the wrong side of the culottes). Align the seam of the waistband with the back central seam of the culottes and stitch to attach.

8 Next, make the elastic cavity. Pull the waistband out from within the culottes and press down 1cm of the waistband and then another 8cm (1–3 years) or 10cm (3–5 years) to the wrong side, ensuring that the folded edge sits just past the stitch line and the seam

allowance is hidden inside the waistband. Pin the first fold line just past the stitch line before pressing the second fold line in place.

9   Remove any pins and open out the waistband again. Take your piece of elastic (see size guide) and pin one end just under the waistband's second (lower) folded edge in line with the outer gather point on the front of the culottes. Pull the elastic around the back of the culottes and attach the other end of the elastic in the same way at the outer gather point on the other side. Run a zigzag stitch back and forth over the ends of the elastic to hold it in place.

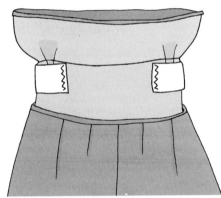

10 Fold the waistband back down and pin once again to ensure that the seam allowance sits inside the waistband, then stitch your waistband closed, pulling the elastic through as you stitch to allow the fabric to sit flat.

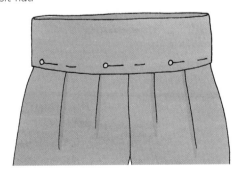

So pretty – and perfect for the girl who likes to cartwheel!

11 Now you need to fix the elastic within the waistband to keep the gathering consistent. Fold your elastic in half to find the centre point, make sure this centre point sits at the centre point of the back of the culottes and pin in place. If you like, you can add another pin on either side to ensure that the top of the elastic sits right up against the top folded edge of the cavity; just make sure that you are pulling out the slack of the fabric so that the elastic stretch is evenly distributed around. Whilst stretching the elastic within the cavity, top stitch 0.5cm down from the top folded edge, from one end of the elastic around the back of the culottes to the other end of the elastic. Repeat this process 0.5cm up from the bottom edge of the elastic so that you have two stitch lines running parallel.

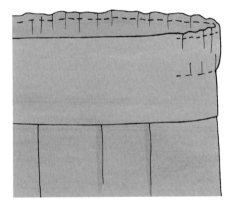

12 Press your lower hems 1cm and then 2cm to the wrong side. Turn the culottes right side out and finish your hems.

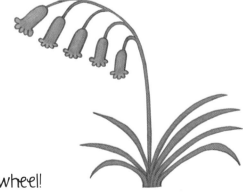

Paw Print Mittens

Level:

Cutting and preparation:
20 mins

Sewing and finishing:
1 hr

You will need:
- Pattern pieces E1 & E2
- Paw print appliqué can be found on page 124
- Matching machine threads
- Standard machine needles and jersey machine needles

Fabric (all measurements are based on largest size):
- 30cm width x 20cm length topside fur (back of hands)
- 30cm width x 20cm length palm side medium-weight fabric (at least one of your outer fabrics, topside or palm side, needs to be stretchy in order for the hand to insert comfortably)
- 15cm width x 30cm length jersey cuffing
- 30cm width x 40cm length jersey lining
- Small piece of leatherette for appliqué patches

Whenever we feel sad, we make mittens. Okay, that's not strictly true, but we should – it's quicker and cheaper than any form of therapy! Here is a simple little project with speedy results that are guaranteed to raise a smile. Kitten's mittens, monster mittens or puppy paws, they are happy to be whatever you want them to be.

Finished garment size guide
Total length:

1–2 years	16cm
2–3 years	17.75cm
3–5 years	19.25cm

FABRIC: These comfy mittens have a faux fur topside matched with a soft velvet palm side. The super-soft stretchy velour lining gives a lovely indulgent and extra cosy finish. A contrasting leatherette works well for the paw prints.

Instructions

1 Trace your pattern pieces, making note of any specific markings or instructions. Don't forget to trace and cut your little paw print patches (see page 124). Lay out the pattern pieces on your fabric and cut.

2 Take your palm side mitten pieces (E1) and lay out your paw print appliqué pieces as desired, bearing in mind the 0.75cm seam allowance around all edges. Attach using appliqué stitch (see page 10).

3 Place your topside fur pieces, right sides facing, on top of the appliquéd palm side pieces and pin in place. Stitch around them leaving just the straight bottom edge open. Turn your mittens right side out and put to one side.

4 Match two of your lining pieces, right sides facing, and stitch around leaving just the bottom straight edge open. Repeat with your other two lining pieces. Insert your linings into the mitten outers, wrong sides facing.

5 Take one cuff piece (E2), fold it in half in the direction of the stretch and stitch to create a stretchy tube of fabric. Repeat with the other cuff piece.

6 Fold each cuff piece in half again, wrong sides facing, so that the remaining raw edges align, then press to create two little cuffs.

7 Take your folded cuffs and insert each one over the end of the main hand piece of the mittens so that all the raw edges meet and the seam of the cuff is aligned with one of the side seams of the mittens. Stitch, taking care to catch all layers; it's fiddly but you are just moments away from seeing the adorable mittens completed, so just go slowly and breathe!

Done! So, mittens for every small person in your life this Christmas?

Cat Ears Headband

Level:

Cutting and preparation:
10 mins

Sewing and finishing:
30 mins

You will need:
- Pattern pieces F1 and F2
- Matching machine threads
- Standard machine needles and jersey machine needles

Fabric (all measurements are based on largest size):
- 50cm width x 20cm length main fabric (stretch jersey)
- A small piece of medium-weight fabric for the ears

FABRIC: The main headband is made from black stretch knit velour and the ears a rich black velvet – when it comes to cat ears this fabric has the perfect qualities, looks really professional and is sturdy enough to hold the upright ear shape well.

When it comes to last minute fancy dress announcements, ears on a headband are the best parenting hack. It's an easy-peasy project and any parent or lovely relative can whip up a headband within the hour. Some kids can be reluctant when it comes to dressing up; no worries, discreetly transform them with a little set of ears whilst collecting a couple of well-earned parenting points for that handmade touch.

Finished garment size guide
Headband total circumference:

1–2 years	40cm
2–3 years	42cm
3–5 years	44cm

Instructions

1 Take two of your ear triangles (F1) and stitch along the two short edges leaving the bottom open. Repeat with your other ear pieces. Turn right side out and use a chopstick to push out the seams. Snip off any excess seam that protrudes along the bottom edge.

2 Mark the centre point of your headband (F2) and position your ears with the bottom raw edge of the ear along one of the long edges of the headband, approximately 2cm either side of the centre point, right sides facing. Switch to jersey needles and use a basting stitch to secure the ears in place.

3 Fold the headband in half lengthways to align the two longest edges and sandwich the ears inside. Use a stretch stitch to close up this long edge.

4 Turn the headband right side out and roll the fabric around so that the seam line sits across the top centre (ears pointing up). Pin or press to hold this line in place.

5 Fold in 1cm on one of the raw edges and insert the opposite raw edge into this by 2cm, pinning in place. Take your headband to the machine and stitch through all the layers of the fabric across the overlap using a zigzag stitch.

Next time you're working on a jersey garment, set aside the remnants for a cute matching headband.

the
Fox

Slim-leg Trousers

Slim-leg trousers are a quick and easy route to an original and stylish looking outfit. Tweed is such a fun fabric to play around with and it brings that wonderful sense of vintage charm to the table.

Level:

Cutting and preparation:
15 mins

Sewing and finishing:
45 mins

You will need:
- Pattern pieces G1 & G2
- Standard machine needles
- 18mm wide elastic
- Matching threads

Fabric (all measurements are based on largest size):
- 1m width x 75cm length medium-weight fabric

FABRIC: These trousers are made in a cotton and wool mix tweed. Tweed comes in so many different colour combinations and it's a great way of injecting a bit of fun and style into an outfit. Just be careful because the more wool-rich options are often a little more scratchy on the skin, which will result in an instant rejection of your hard work!

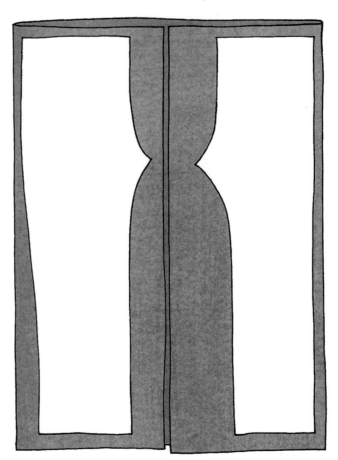

Finished garment size guide
Outer leg length:

12–18 months	47.75cm
18–24 months	51.5cm
2–3 years	55.25cm
3–4 years	59.5cm
4–5 years	64cm

**Waist circumference
(elastic measurement):**

12–18 months	42cm
18–24 months	44cm
2–3 years	46cm
3–4 years	48cm
4–5 years	50cm

Instructions

1   Trace your pattern pieces, making note of any specific markings or instructions. Lay out the pattern pieces on your fabric and cut.

2   Take one of your front leg pieces (G1) with the corresponding back piece (G2) and attach down the outer leg side seam, right sides facing. Next, align the inner leg seams and stitch from the crotch to the bottom of the leg. It is worth reinforcing around the inner leg crotch by running a line of stitching very close to the original seam for added strength.

3   Repeat this entire process to join your other two front and back leg pieces.

4   Turn one of your legs right side out and place inside the other leg, right sides facing, with the inner leg seams aligned. Stitch from the centre of the top, around the crotch (aligning seams) and up the other side.

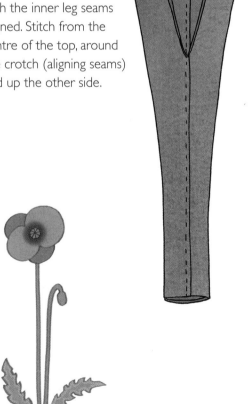

5   Turn the trousers inside out and press 1cm and then another 2cm to the wrong side at the waist hem to make your elastic cavity. Cut your required amount of elastic (see size guide) and use a zigzag stitch to connect the two ends of your elastic with a small overlap, creating a loop of elastic.

6   Insert your loop of elastic into the waist cavity. Close the cavity by stitching close to the folded edge, taking care not to catch the elastic. Pull the elastic through as you stitch to spread the gathering and allow the hem to sit flat.

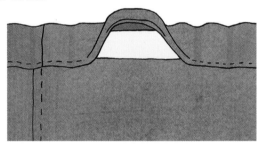

7   Press your ankle hems 1cm and then 2cm to the wrong side. Turn the trousers right side out and finish your hems (it is easier to pass the ankles through the machine with the trousers right side out).

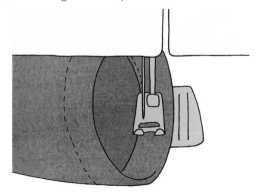

You can never have
too many pairs of trousers,
so why not whip up several
more pairs in different
fabrics?

Fox Face Dungarees

Level:

Cutting and preparation:
20 mins

Sewing and finishing:
1–2 hrs

You will need:
- Pattern pieces H1 & H2
- Fox face appliqué can be found on page 122
- 2 small black buttons for appliqué eyes (6–8mm)
- Matching threads
- Standard machine needles
- Black embroidery thread
- Embroidery needle
- 40mm wide elastic
- 2 or 4 large buttons for fastening straps

Fabric (all measurements are based on largest size):
- 1.4m width x 1.2m length medium- to heavy-weight fabric
- 1.4m width x 1.2m length light-weight lining fabric, such as cotton
- A small piece of white leatherette or felt
- A small square of orange boiled wool or felt

If there was an award for cutest garment type, dungarees would win hands down. They are playful, comfy and unisex, the perfect embodiment of the innocence of childhood. And our foxy dungarees have a little secret; Mr Fox isn't just for looking at. He's actually a pocket for stashing away secret things like sweets, jewels and frogs.

A note on cutting appliqué shapes: The appliqué shapes for this project can be found on page 122. If you're using leatherette it is easiest to draw the pattern shape onto the back of the fabric and then cut to get a really neat shape. This should work well for most fabrics, especially with small pieces.

Finished garment size guide
**Shoulder to floor length
(lowest button setting):**

12–18 months	69cm
18–24 months	75cm
2–3 years	81cm
3–4 years	87cm
4–5 years	93cm

Chest circumference:

12–18 months	59cm
18–24 months	61cm
2–3 years	63cm
3–4 years	65cm
4–5 years	67cm

FABRIC: Here the dungarees are made with a good-quality cotton-rich velvet outer fabric with a matching brown cotton poplin lining. Other nice options for the outer fabric include corduroy or a soft denim. Although usually quite expensive, moleskin is also a beautiful fabric for this type of garment. The lining is a great way to inject a bit of fun with a colourful print and it's very easy to add on extra leg length to the pattern to allow for a chunky turn up to properly show off your lining.

Instructions

1   Trace your pattern pieces, making note of any specific markings or instructions. Don't forget to trace and cut your fox face appliqué pieces (see page 122). Lay out the pattern pieces on your fabric and cut.

2   First you need to make the little fox face appliqué/ pocket. Position your white leatherette fox cheek and inner ear pieces onto your front outer fox face and pin in place, leaving a border of 1cm plus an additional 0.5cm around the ear. Use a standard straight stitch to attach. Lay out your black button eyes and attach (see page 10).

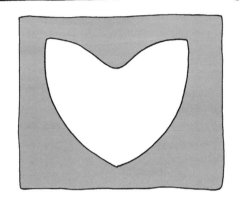

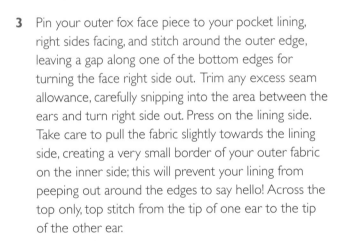

3 Pin your outer fox face piece to your pocket lining, right sides facing, and stitch around the outer edge, leaving a gap along one of the bottom edges for turning the face right side out. Trim any excess seam allowance, carefully snipping into the area between the ears and turn right side out. Press on the lining side. Take care to pull the fabric slightly towards the lining side, creating a very small border of your outer fabric on the inner side; this will prevent your lining from peeping out around the edges to say hello! Across the top only, top stitch from the tip of one ear to the tip of the other ear.

4 Take your outer front body pieces (H1) and put them together, right sides facing, and stitch down the central seam from the top of the front to the point of the crotch. Place your fox pocket centrally on the chest with the tips of the ears 6cm below the top edge. Pin and top stitch from the point of one ear around the bottom of the face and up the other side, taking care to close up the gap you used for turning. Return to each of the top corners of the pocket and run a few stitches diagonally across each ear tip for added strength. To complete the appliqué, take your black embroidery thread and stitch a little nose at the tip of your fox face.

5 Attach your two back outer pieces (H2) as with the front – down the central seam to the point of the crotch. Grab your elastic and mark out a 10cm length, leaving a few centimetres each side of this for stitching allowance, then mark the centre point. On your back outer piece, measure 2cm up from the bottom of the armholes and mark at the centre with chalk. Measure along this line 7.5cm either side of the seam. You are going to stretch the 10cm elastic along this 15cm line to create a gather. Use a zigzag stitch to fasten each side of the elastic in place where you marked 7.5cm out from the seam and then revert to a standard straight stitch to stitch across the top and bottom of the elastic, pulling the elastic taut as you go to allow the fabric to sit flat.

6 Attach your front and back outer body pieces down each side from the underarm down to the ankle. Next, stitch from one of the inner ankle points up the inside leg and down the other side, aligning the crotch seams. It's worth reinforcing the crotch as it'll need to accommodate a lot of bending and stretching.

7 As with the outer body pieces, attach your lining front and back pieces down the central seams and then attach at the sides and around the inner leg.

8 Insert your lining into the outer body, right sides facing. Stitch across the top front edge and then begin to work your way around the entire top raw edges, coming around the underarm (aligning side seams), around the straps and up the other side. Again, it's a good idea to reinforce the underarm area. Reach up into one of the legs and pull the whole garment through to turn right side out and push the lining back through the outer dungarees. Press the seams flat. Turn the garment inside out to press both fabrics at the ankle hems, 1cm and then 2cm to the wrong side. Stitch around both ankle hems.

9 Now all that's left to do are the buttons and buttonholes. Start with the buttonholes. Measure out and mark with chalk where you'd like the buttonholes to sit on the front bib section. Attach the buttonhole foot and amend your machine settings accordingly. Place the fabric so that the start of the stitching will be around 1cm from the side seam and go for it. Repeat on the other side. If you want to allow for a bit of growing room, include two sets of buttons, placed 2cm and 6cm from the end of the strap (the full-length measurements given are based on this positioning). Go ahead and attach your buttons (see page 10). Carefully take your seam ripper and open up your buttonholes – a pin placed across one end of the buttonhole creates the perfect barrier to prevent accidentally ripping out the other side.

Next time, why not have a go at designing your own little appliqué face?

Fox Duffle Coat

Level:

Cutting and preparation:
1–2 hrs

Sewing and finishing:
8–10 hrs

You will need:
- Pattern pieces B1–B3, B5–B8, B12–B19, I1–I8
- 4 toggles
- 2 large buttons
- 1m cording
- Matching machine threads
- Standard machine needles
- Snap popper fastener tool
- 4 sets of snap popper fastener inserts

Fabric (all measurements are based on largest size):
- 1.5m width x 1.5m length outer main fabric
- 1.5m width x 1.1m length lining fabric
- 1m width x 50cm length outer accent fabric (faux fur)
- 50cm width x 50cm length leatherette

Mr Fox is a sneaky opportunist who will raid the biscuit tin 'til it's empty. He has a bright and cheeky spirit that helps to connect us with our own sense of mischief. This fox coat embodies this creature so well: with big alert ears and a statement bushy tail, he is splendid and proud. This design was our first animal-inspired clothing creation, and we absolutely love it.

Before you begin:
This is a big project; you're going to be working with a lot of pattern pieces and fabric, so it's important to be super organised from the start. Try to organise your pieces as the sections of the coat; so put all the hood pieces in a pile, all the linings bits, sleeves, etc., or you may prefer to just sort them according to fabric type. It's also a good idea to keep the pattern pieces with their corresponding fabric pieces so that when they are referred to by reference number in the instructions here, you know which piece to grab.

A note on cutting fur and leatherette:
For the leatherette it is easiest to draw the pattern shape onto the back of the fabric multiple times and then cut to get a really consistent shape. With the fur, it's a good idea to place the pattern on the wrong side of the fabric and cut out rather than trying to get a clean cut line amongst a deep pile of fur.

Finished garment size guide

Collar to bottom hem length:

1–2 years	37.25cm
2–3 years	40.5cm
3–4 years	43.75cm
4–5 years	47cm

Chest circumference:

1–2 years	68cm
2–3 years	70cm
3–4 years	72cm
4–5 years	74cm

FABRIC: This fox coat is made with 100% cotton fine corduroy outer fabric with a medium-weight cotton poplin lining. The faux fur and leatherette add nice touches as accent fabrics. You can have a lot of fun with whatever combinations you choose, exploring colour, texture and fabric weights. For your first attempt, keep things really simple, but once you've successfully produced your first coat, why not mix it up a bit and try out something different, like a textured lining or water-repellent outer?

Fox Duffle Coat   61

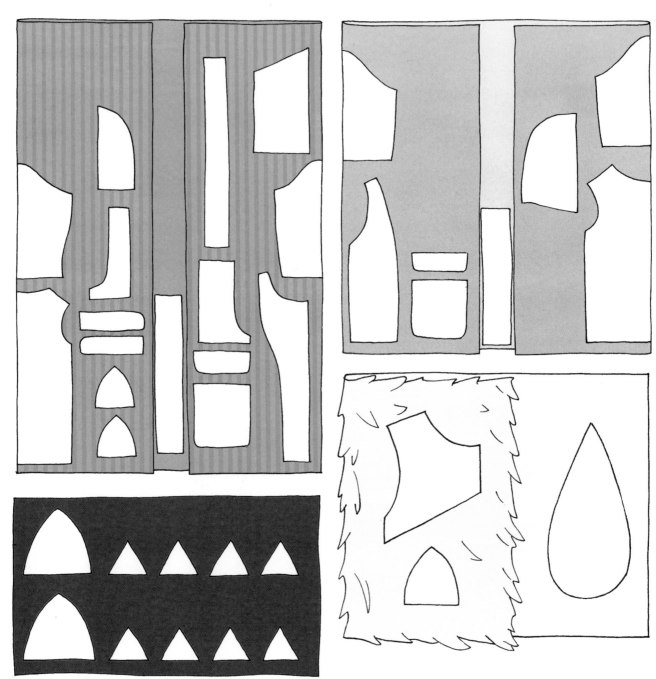

Instructions

1 Trace your pattern pieces, making note of any specific markings or instructions. Sort your pattern pieces into piles according to fabric type, then lay out pieces on your fabric and cut.

2 Begin with the outer body pieces. Pin the bottom diagonal edge of one of your outer front upper panels (B1) to the corresponding diagonal edge of the outer front lower panel (B2) and attach. Top stitch the seam allowance onto the lower front body piece approximately 0.5cm from the seam. Repeat with the other side. Take your outer front centre panels (B3) and attach each one to the front centre raw edge of the main body pieces. Top stitch the seam allowance towards the front centre panels.

3 Place your tail appliqué piece (I1) onto your outer back piece (B5), centrally aligned and 7cm up from the bottom raw edge. Pin securely in place. Use your chosen appliqué stitch (see page 10) and a thread that corresponds with the colour of the tail fabric to carefully stitch around the edge of the tail, taking care not to stitch onto the main fabric to keep the edge neat.

4 Stitch together your front and back outer pieces at the shoulders, right sides facing.

5 Take your four cuff pieces (I2) and pair them, right sides facing. Stitch around the edge, leaving just the shortest straight edge open. Trim the seam allowance around the curve. Take a chopstick and carefully push the cuff pieces right side out. Press flat.

6 Place your pressed cuff pieces with the short raw edge at the side of each outer sleeve (B19) approximately 7cm from the bottom edge of the sleeve. Make sure that with the arms lying side by side you have created a mirror image resulting in a left and a right sleeve. Pin securely in place and top stitch to attach. Position your two large buttons in the centre of the curved end of the cuff strap and attach.

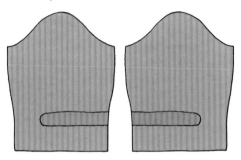

7 Align the curved edge of each outer sleeve with the curve of the armholes on your outer body piece, right sides facing; pin together, ensuring that the centre of the sleeve lines up with the shoulder seam, and stitch to attach. Make sure that you are affixing the correct sleeve to the correct armhole; the button on the cuff strap should sit towards the back of the body.

8 Fold each sleeve in half lengthways, right sides facing, and stitch along the raw edges, continuing down the side of the body, ensuring that the underarm seams align. You might like to reinforce the underarm area as it's a notorious danger zone for holes!

The Fox, the Bear & the Bunny

9 Lay each of your pocket lining pieces (B7 – lining fabric) onto the pocket outer pieces (B7 – main fabric), right sides facing, and stitch, leaving just the top straight edge open. Trim excess seam allowance around the curved corners and turn right side out. Repeat the same process with each of the two pocket flaps (B8). Press all of the pocket pieces, taking care to pull the fabric slightly towards the lining side, creating a very small border of your outer fabric on the inner side (this will prevent your lining peeping around the edge when top stitching later). Press a 1cm seam inwardly to the wrong side of the fabrics along the top edge of your two main pocket pieces. Stitch across this top edge. Take your pocket flaps and finish the raw edge of both fabrics together with a zigzag or edging stitch, then press 0.75cm to the lining side across this top edge.

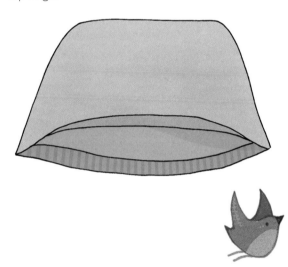

10 With your coat outer body laid right side up, position and pin your two main pockets in place, measuring approximately 7cm up from the bottom straight edge and 11cm in from the front centre raw edge. Top stitch around each pocket and then return to each of the top corners and run a few stitches diagonally across each side for added strength. Pin your two pocket flaps in place with the folded finished edge 0.75cm up from the top of the main pocket, allow it to close over and top stitch across the top straight edge.

11 Now make the hood. Grab all of your hood and ear pieces, ready to start on the ears first. Before you begin, make sure that you have to hand the threads to match both your inner and middle ear fabric pieces. Take one of your outer ear pieces (I3) and one middle ear accent fabric piece (I4) and centrally align them at the bottom edge. With matching thread, use an appliqué stitch to attach (see page 10). Next, change your thread colour and take your inner ear piece (I5), again centrally align along the bottom edge and use the appliqué stitch to attach. Repeat for the other ear. Lay both of your remaining two outer ear pieces flat and place each of your appliquéd ear fronts on top, right sides facing. Stitch around, leaving just the bottom straight edge open. Turn your ears right side out and push out the seams with a chopstick. Press on the non-appliquéd side (don't melt your leatherette!). How cute do they look?!

12 Next, make the main part of the hood. With your hood outer back panel (I6) laid right side up, position one of your finished ear pieces, appliquéd side up, approximately 2cm from the top with the straight bottom edge of the ear lying along the straight front edge of the hood piece. Place the hood outer front panel (I7) on top of this, right side down, sandwiching the ear between the front and back panels. Pin along the long straight edge and stitch, ensuring that you catch all of the layers. Repeat for the other side with your corresponding hood and ear pieces. With right sides facing, pin the long straight edge of the hood outer central panel (B12) along the curved edge of the outer hood section and stitch from the top front of the hood all the way down to the bottom. Pin the other side of the central panel in the same way to the other side of the hood so that the strip joins the two sides of the hood together.

13 For the hood lining, lay your hood inner central strip (B13) along the curved edge of one of the hood inner back panels (B14) and as with the outer pieces, pin and stitch. Repeat for the other side so that the centre strip joins the two sides of the hood together. Take your hood inner front panels (B15 – main fabric) and stitch together, right sides facing, along the top short straight edge. Open out and lay the long straight edge, right sides facing, along the entire front edge of the hood lining pieces. Pin and stitch. Place the hood lining into the hood outer, right sides facing, aligning the front edges, and stitch. Turn right sides out, press around the front edge of the hood and top stitch this front edge.

14 Now you're ready to attach the hood to the coat outer body. Find the central point of the base of the hood and pin, outer sides facing, to the back centre of the neckline of the coat. Continue to pin around securely and attach.

15 Before you bring all of the components together into one awesome fox coat you need to complete the lining. Place one of your front inner side panels (B16), right sides facing, against your corresponding front inner middle panel (B17 – main fabric). Pin together along the long curved edge and stitch. Repeat for the other side. Attach the shoulder (top short edge) of each of these to the corresponding shoulder of the inner back piece (B18). Open out your now-attached lining and pin the top curve of the sleeve lining (B6) into the armhole curve, ensuring that the centre of the sleeve sits at the shoulder seam. Attach and repeat for the other side.

16 Fold each lining sleeve in half lengthways, right sides facing, and stitch along the raw edges, continuing down the side of the body, ensuring that the underarm seams align. As with the outer pieces, reinforce this stitch just around the underarm area.

17 If you are going to use popper fasteners in your coat, now is the time to insert them. Lay out your coat outer and use a chalk pencil to mark the positioning for your poppers on the front centre panel of the child's left side (right side to look at). Sit the first popper fairly close to the top, so it provides a nice snug seal against the cold, remembering to leave seam allowance. Then position three more poppers at regular intervals down the coat, taking the last popper no lower than the mid-point of the pocket; remember to leave space for a hem plus the leatherette triangles. The poppers for the other side of the coat will go on the lining piece, so be sure to align the top edges of the lining and outer body pieces to transfer your

markings across to the child's right side of the lining piece. There is a 4cm difference in length between the lining and outer pieces so it is important that your poppers line up from the top edge and not the bottom. Now insert your popper fasteners. Be warned, you do not want to make a mistake at this stage, so check and check again that you have correctly aligned your poppers.

18 Pin your lining, right sides facing, to the neckline of the outer body section, taking care to align them at the shoulder seams. Stitch around the neck opening to sandwich your hood in between these layers. This is probably the trickiest part of this project, just put in a lot of pins, take it slow and you will be just fine.

19 Sometimes you can be left with a bit of a wonky line running across the entire bottom width of your outer and lining body pieces where all the different pieces have joined. If this is the case, take your scissors and tidy it up, but note that the lining is intended to be 4cm shorter than the outer body section so please don't chop this off! Take measurements to compare each side in length so that you aren't left with one side of the coat hanging slightly lower than the other, it's an easy mistake to make and it's so disappointing to discover right at the last moment. Now that you have a lovely straight line to work with, pin together the outer and lining body pieces, right sides facing, along the bottom raw edge and stitch 2cm in from the edge.

20 Take one side of your coat and stitch the front central edge closed starting from the top. When you reach the bottom, the outer coat will pull around by 2cm towards the lining side; continue to stitch through this overlap whilst pulling the seam allowance downwards so that it will sit inside the hem. Take the other side and instead of closing this up entirely, leave a large gap for pulling the entire coat right side out. Begin stitching from the top and part way down, leave your gap, then resume stitching, ensuring that you are left with the same 2cm overlap at the bottom as before. Carefully trim the two top corners to remove any bulk from the collar.

21 Reach inside the gap that you have left and begin to turn your garment. Take your chopstick/pencil and push out all the corners. Press your coat starting at the front seams. On the side that you have left open, carefully fold in the same seam allowance along the gap, keeping a consistent straight edge.

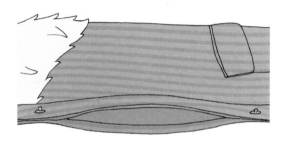

22 When pressing along the bottom hem, reach back inside the lining to make sure the 2cm seam allowance is pushed downwards to sit within the hem and pin this in place. Top stitch a 1cm hem across the entire bottom of the coat and then top stitch the two front edges, closing your turning gap as you go.

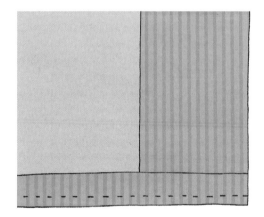

23 Push your outer body sleeve through the sleeve lining so that your sleeve is inside out. Press 1cm of the outer sleeve towards the wrong side and another 2cm towards the wrong side to make your sleeve hem. The edge of the lining should sit fully inside this hem. Repeat on the other side. Turn the sleeves right side out and top stitch the hem.

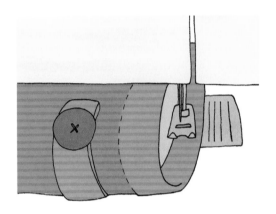

25 Finally, take your 8 leatherette triangles (18) and use a standard straight stitch to top stitch them over the raw ends of the cording on each side of the coat. It helps to disguise the under-stitching if you use a coordinating thread on top whilst keeping the bobbin the same colour as the main body of the coat.

This is a great project that appeals to both girls and boys, and the autumnal colours make it perfect for when the colder weather begins.

24 Cut eight 12cm lengths of cording and insert four of them through your chosen toggles. Place to one side. Lay out your coat and pin or mark with chalk where you'd like your toggles to be. For a really good seal down the front of the coat, position the toggles in between the poppers. Affix your toggles to the coat with a small reinforced stitch on the child's left side. Attach your remaining loops of cording to the opposite side, making sure they line up with the toggles.

the Mouse

Long-sleeved T-shirt

Level:

Cutting and preparation:
30 mins

Sewing and finishing:
1–2 hrs

You will need:
- Pattern pieces J1–J4
- Jersey machine needles
- Matching threads

Fabric (all measurements are based on largest size):
- 1m x 1m of stretch jersey fabric

FABRIC: Stretchy fabric is essential for this project; the T-shirt shown is made from a 95% cotton, 5% elastene knit jersey fabric in a bright and happy yellow and white stripe. Elastane has brilliant elastic properties and allows jersey garments to hold their shape well even after being stretched. Another option is 100% cotton knit jersey fabric which is also lovely and completely natural.

Formed in 'cheddar yellow' for the mouse section, this long sleeved T-shirt is easy to adapt to ensure that you can build entire homemade outfits of your own. A must-have pattern for your collection and the perfect excuse to splash out on fun jersey fabric.

Before you begin:
- Failing to use the fabric-appropriate needles may result in the fabric laddering at the seams, so make sure you use jersey needles.
- As with all the patterns in this book, a 0.75cm seam allowance has been included here. If you are using an overlocker machine there is no need to trim off any excess as the distance between the needles and blade of the machine should be about 0.75cm.
- Pin plenty – stretch fabrics like to move around!
- When feeding the fabric through the machine take care not to pull or stretch it, this would disfigure your garment and cause the pattern pieces to become unaligned. Let the machine do the work.
- Jersey fabric won't fray so there's no need to finish the raw edges on a sewing machine.

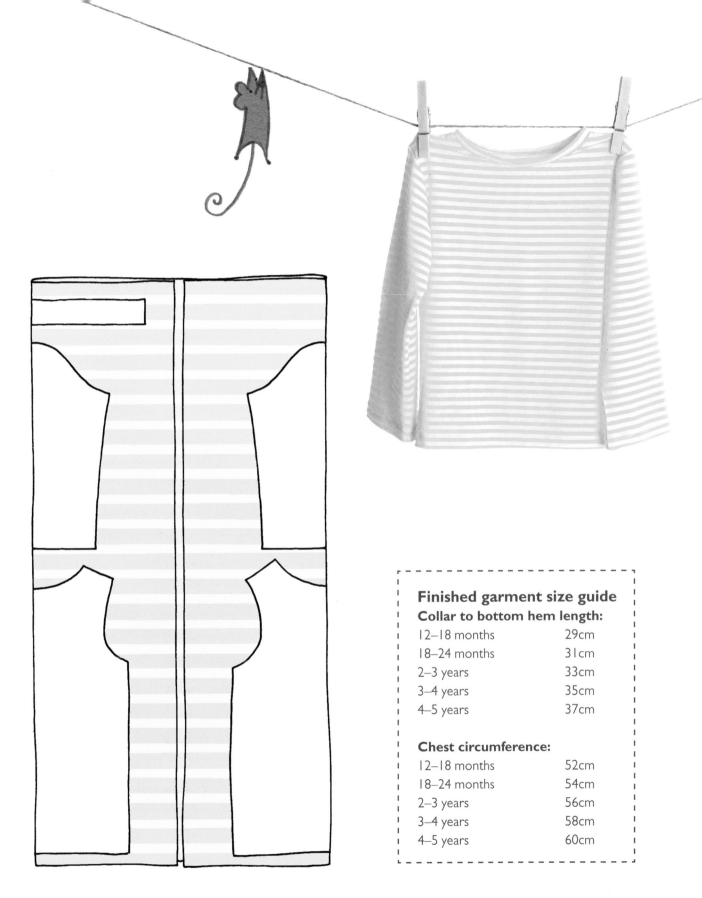

Finished garment size guide
Collar to bottom hem length:

12–18 months	29cm
18–24 months	31cm
2–3 years	33cm
3–4 years	35cm
4–5 years	37cm

Chest circumference:

12–18 months	52cm
18–24 months	54cm
2–3 years	56cm
3–4 years	58cm
4–5 years	60cm

The Fox, the Bear & the Bunny

Instructions

1. Trace your pattern pieces, making note of any specific markings or instructions. Lay out the pattern pieces on your fabric and cut.

2. Set your sewing machine to a stretch stitch or set up your overlocker, if you have one.

3. Lay out the body front and back pieces (J1 & J2), right sides facing, and stitch them together along both shoulder edges.

4. Take your neck edging strip (J3) and stitch together the two short edges, right sides facing, to create a continuous loop of fabric. Fold this loop in half lengthways with wrong sides facing and press to create your neck piece.

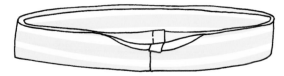

5. Open out the front and back of the T-shirt and lay it flat, right side up. Pin your neck loop into the neck hole with raw edges aligned and the seam of the neck loop pinned at one of the shoulder seams.

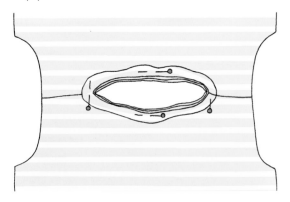

6. Sew around the neck hole, taking extra care not to stretch the fabric as you stitch or you will end up with an ugly loose neck hole. Remove pins as you work or your machine is going to get really angry with you! Press the seam flat inwardly.

7. Take one of the sleeve pieces (J4) and pin the curved edge of the sleeve into the curve of the armhole, right sides facing. Make sure the centre of the sleeve curve sits at the shoulder seam. Stitch together and then repeat with the second sleeve.

8. Take one side of the now fully attached garment and fold the sleeve in half, right sides facing. Align the raw edge all the way from the cuff right down the entire side of the garment to the bottom edge. Stitch together. Take it slowly as you stitch around the armpit curve – this a real danger zone for not properly catching both pieces of fabric, which results in nasty holes. Repeat on the other side.

9. Now all that's left to do is finish the hems. On each sleeve edge, and along the bottom of the garment, press a 2cm hem to the wrong side. If you are the lucky owner of a cover stitch machine, finish the hems using your glorious stitch. If using a sewing machine, stitch around just inside the raw edge using a stretch stitch. Don't use a straight stitch here or as soon as the child pushes their little hand through the hole the threads will snap, and nobody wants that.

There you go, one lovely fitted long-sleeved T-shirt, simple and versatile.

Mouse Pocket Pinafore Dress

Level:

Cutting and preparation:
20 mins

Sewing and finishing:
1–2 hrs

You will need:
- Pattern pieces K1–K4
- Mouse appliqué can be found on page 124
- Two small black beads (2mm)
- Embroidery thread – white and pink
- Embroidery needle
- Matching machine threads
- Standard machine needles
- 2 or 3 small buttons

Fabric (all measurements are based on largest size):
- 1.2m x 1.2m light- to medium-weight fabric, such as cotton poplin or linen
- A small piece of felt for main appliqué plus a contrasting piece of fabric for inner ear pieces

This little mouse dress is our interpretation of a simple and classic A-line style. We love the overall simplicity paired with the cute but subtle pocket appliqué. With a change of fabric, this sweet dress is easily transformed from play clothes to party frock.

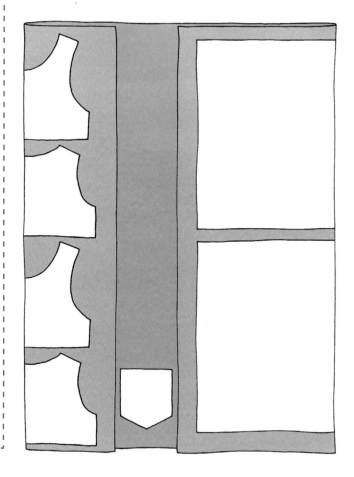

Finished garment size guide
Collar to bottom hem length:

12–18 months	43cm
18–24 months	46.75cm
2–3 years	50.5cm
3–4 years	54.75cm
4–5 years	59cm

Chest circumference:

12–18 months	55cm
18–24 months	57cm
2–3 years	59cm
3–4 years	61cm
4–5 years	63cm

FABRIC: The medium-weight linen-style grey cotton fabric used here is thick enough to be sturdy yet still soft and comfortable. This dress works wonderfully in brightly patterned cotton poplins, too. For the little mouse appliqué use darker grey felt and tiny pieces of cotton poplin for the inner ears. If using cottons for appliqué work, take care to avoid fraying and be sure to stitch down thoroughly with your zigzag stitch.

A note on cutting appliqué shapes: The appliqué shapes for this project can be found on page 124. It is usually easiest to draw the pattern shape onto the back of the fabric and then cut to get a really neat shape. This should work well for most fabrics, especially with small pieces.

Mouse Pocket Pinafore Dress

Instructions

1 Trace your pattern pieces, making note of any specific markings or instructions. Don't forget to trace and cut your mouse face appliqué pieces (see page 124). Lay out the pattern pieces on your fabric and cut. When cutting the bodice front and back pieces you may like to choose an alternative fabric for the lining, something lighter weight, maybe a fun complimentary print in cotton poplin.

2 Start with the appliqué. Take one of the mouse outer ear pieces and one inner ear piece. Attach the inner ear piece onto the centre of the outer ear piece using your chosen appliqué stitch (see page 10). Repeat with the other ear pieces.

3 Take your mouse face piece and mark the centre at the bottom of the face for the nose to be stitched, remember to leave space for the zigzag stitch that you will use to attach the appliqué to the actual garment. For the nose you could use a bright pink embroidery thread, as here, making just a few stitches back and forth to create a nose shape – four or five stitches should be adequate. Fasten the embroidery thread at the back of the work with a small knot, which will become hidden. For the eyes, use tiny 2mm black beads or just some thread. Position the eyes by sight and stitch to attach to the main mouse face, you will add whiskers later.

4 Now prepare the pocket. Fold the top edge of your pocket piece (K1) to the wrong side by 1cm, press, then turn another 1cm and press again. Stitch across this top edge.

5 Fold and press the side and bottom edges of the pocket by 1cm to the wrong side so that all the raw edges are tucked away.

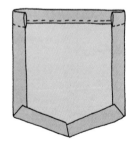

6 Lay out one of the skirt pieces (K2) right side up with the longest edge horizontal. Place your pocket and mouse onto the skirt piece as desired, remembering your 3cm hem allowance and 0.75cm side seam. In the dress pictured, which is size 2–3 years, the pocket is positioned on the right-hand side, 10cm from the bottom raw edge and 8cm from the side edge. Pin and stitch the pocket in place, adding a little stitch diagonally across each top corner of the pocket to make it extra secure – kids' clothing needs to be robust!

7 Now add our little mouse peeking out of the pocket. Peel back the top lip of the pocket and pin this out of the way. Use chalk to mark a line where you want the mouse face to sit. Place and stitch your mouse face appliqué using the zigzag stitch as before. When stitching, go across the bottom straight line of the face to fasten it in place and then work slowly around the curve of the face. Next position and fasten the ears.

8 For the final stage of the mouse appliqué, take your white embroidery thread for the whiskers. Bring the needle through from the wrong side of the fabric at the nose and work 3 large straight stitches out from the nose, then repeat on the other side. Place your appliquéd skirt piece to one side.

9 Attach your outer front bodice piece (K3) and your left and right back pattern pieces (K4) at the shoulders, right sides facing. Repeat with the lining.

10 Lay your now attached outer body pieces and lining pieces together, right sides facing, and pin. Stitch together from the bottom inner edge of the back pieces up the back, around the neckline (ensuring shoulder seams align), then back down the other inner edge of the back piece.

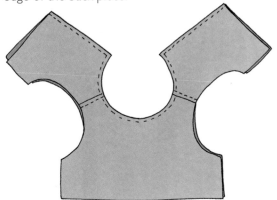

11 Stitch around the armhole curve on both sides.

12 Now turn the bodice right side out. Pull one side of the back section through the shoulder and out the other side. Repeat on the other side.

13 Your bodice should now be right side out (a chopstick is incredibly useful for poking into the corners and making them really crisp). Press all of your seams.

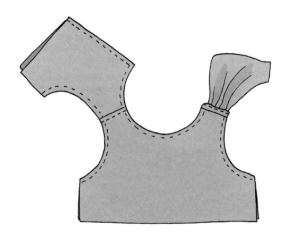

14 Open out the straight raw edges at one side of the back and place, right sides facing, against the corresponding raw side edge of the front, ensuring that the seams at the bottom of the armhole align. Pin together and stitch the side seams all the way from the bottom of the front pieces to the bottom of the back, closing the armhole. Repeat on the other side.

15 Next, position the buttons and buttonholes. Decide how many buttons you'd like to feature on the back of the dress, for a size 2–3-year dress (as pictured) we've used two little wooden buttons. First make the buttonholes. Measure out and mark with chalk where you'd like the centre of your buttons to sit, transfer any markings to the other side, allowing a 2cm centre cross-over on the pattern. Attach your sewing machine buttonhole foot and amend the machine settings accordingly. Place the fabric of the back central seam so that the start of the stitch will be around 0.5cm in from the finished edge then, stitch your buttonhole. Repeat for any other buttonholes.

16 Carefully take your seam ripper and open up your buttonholes – a pin placed across one end of the buttonhole creates the perfect barrier to prevent accidentally ripping out the other side! If you do experience this catastrophe, you can repair it with a zigzag stitch using your sewing machine's feed dogs set down, or repair by hand stitching, it's not the end of the world.

17 Attach your button(s) on the other side of the bodice (see page 10). Button up your bodice pieces and at the bottom, where there is no button, use a pin to hold the 2cm overlap firmly in place.

18 Take your skirt pieces, lay them right sides facing and attach down one short edge (side seam).

19 Set your machine to its maximum stitch length to create a basting stitch. Run this stitch along the raw top edge of the entire width of the two skirt pieces attached and gather each side of the skirt to match the width of the bottom raw edge of the bodice (see page 10) – leave 3–5cm ungathered at each side of the skirt to centralise the gathering.

20 Stitch down the remaining open short edge (side seam) of the skirt pieces.

21 Place your bodice into the skirt, right sides facing, so that the bottom raw edge of the bodice is aligned with the top gathered raw edge of the skirt – make sure that the front of the bodice is facing the front of the skirt (pocket side). Align side seams and pin, then remove the pin from the back of the body piece, making sure you preserve the overlap and re-pin through the skirt. Stitch to attach your skirt to your bodice, removing pins as you go to avoid upsetting your sewing machine.

22 To finish, press the bottom hem 1cm to the wrong side and again by 2cm and sew.

If you like, you can swap the mouse for another little creature peeking out of the pocket.

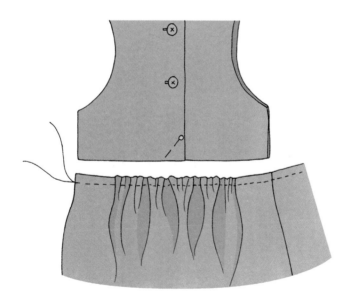

Mouse Capelet

With its ditsy floral lining and gentle grey tone, we pay homage to the sweet and dainty nature of the mouse. Change to black, you have a rat, or tweak the ears and there's a cat. A much quicker project than a full coat with lots of potential to explore your own creative ideas.

Level:

Cutting and preparation:
30 mins

Sewing and finishing:
2–3 hrs

You will need:
- Pattern pieces L1–L12
- Standard machine needles
- Matching threads
- A small length of ribbon

Fabric (all measurements are based on largest size):
- 60cm length x 1.5m width outer main fabric
- 50cm length x 1m width lining fabric
- A small piece of pink felt for the ears

Finished garment size guide

Collar to bottom hem length:

1–2 years	11.75cm
2–3 years	12.25cm
3–4 years	12.75cm
4–5 years	13.25cm

Shoulder width (across back):

1–2 years	30.5cm
2–3 years	31.5cm
3–4 years	32.5cm
4–5 years	33.5cm

FABRIC: The outer fabric here is synthetic coat-grade felt and the lining is a lightweight cotton poplin. The inner ear pieces are made from craft felt – using a synthetic felt adds a touch more complexity to the project because you cannot press the fabric as it will melt! If you use a synthetic felt then instead of pressing you will need to top stitch all of your seams. There's lots of extra pinning at each stage this way – it looks really lovely but it does take a bit more time. The lining here is a pretty yellow floral; it's a great opportunity for sneaking in a bit of fun or an extra cute factor in your fabric choices.

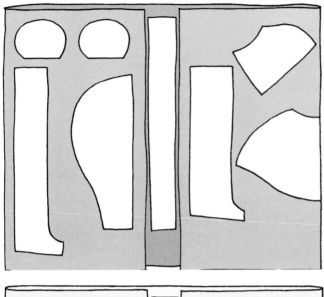

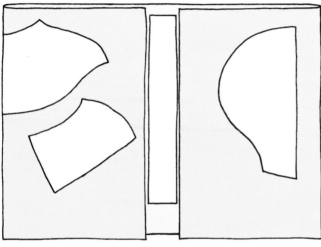

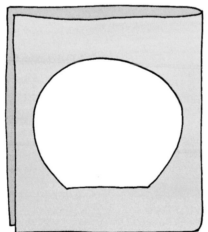

Instructions

1   Trace your pattern pieces, making note of any specific markings or instructions. Lay out the pattern pieces on your fabric and cut.

2   Start with the hood. Take two of your outer ear pieces (L1) and use your appliqué stitch (see page 10) to attach the inner ear pieces (L2), centrally aligned at the bottom edges. Take your other two outer ear pieces and pair each with a front ear piece, right sides facing. Stitch around each ear, leaving the bottom straight edge open. Cut into the seam allowance to remove bulk and turn right side out.

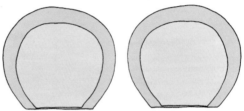

3   Fold your finished ear in half, front sides facing, pinch 1cm of fabric and pin. Stitch to hold this pinch in place, making sure that the fold lies in the opposite direction for each ear to create a mirrored pair.

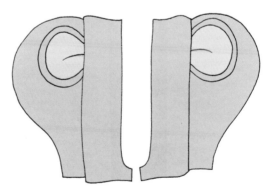

4   With your outer hood back piece (L3) right side up, position one of your finished ear pieces approximately 2cm from the top, with the straight bottom edge

of the ear lying along the straight front edge of the hood piece. Place the outer hood front piece (L4) on top of this, right side down, to sandwich the ear in between. Pin all the layers along the long straight edge and stitch. Repeat for the other side with your corresponding hood and ear sections.

5   Pin your outer hood central panel (L5), right sides facing, along the top curved edge of the outer hood sections. Stitch from the top front of the hood all the way down to the bottom, taking care not to nip the top of your mouse ear (ouch!). Pin the other side of the strip in the same way to the other side of the hood so that the strip joins the two sides of the hood together.

6   Lay your inner hood central panel (L6) along the curved edge of the inner hood back panel (L7) and as with the outer pieces, pin and stitch. Repeat for the other side so that the centre strip joins the two sides of the hood lining together. Take your inner hood front panels (L8 – main fabric) and stitch together, right sides facing, along the top short straight edge. Open out and lay the long straight edge, right sides facing, along the entire front edge of the hood lining. Pin and stitch. Place the hood lining into the hood outer, right sides facing, aligning the front edges and stitch. Turn right sides out, press around the front edge of the hood and top stitch this front edge.

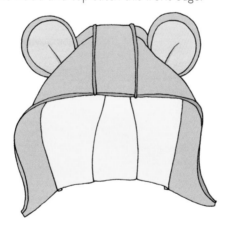

7   Take your back outer piece (L9) and attach it to each of the front outer pieces (L10) along the shoulder edges. Repeat this process with your lining pieces (L11 and L12).

8   Pin your hood to the capelet outer with outer fabrics facing, aligning the centre point of the hood with the central point at the back of the capelet. Attach, taking care to catch all of the layers.

9   Pin your lining, right sides facing, to the neck line of the outer body section, taking care to align at the centre back and shoulder seams. Stitch around the neck opening in order to sandwich your hood in between these layers.

10 Align the bottom edge of the outer body with the bottom edge of the capelet lining, right sides facing. It helps to roll up the hood so that it lies nicely inside with the ears out of harm's way. Pin at the seams and then continue to pin thoroughly in between. Stitch 0.5cmm in around the entire bottom edge.

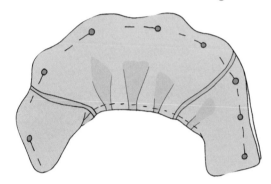

11 Reach inside one of the open edges and carefully and gradually pull the hood, followed by the entire garment, to turn right side out.

12 Press and pin the bottom hem, pulling it 0.5cm around to the lining side. Top stitch across the bottom edge leaving around 2cm unstitched at either end.

13 Fold in 1cm of both outer and lining fabrics down the two front centre open edges, press and pin. Cut two lengths of ribbon and finish one edge of each by folding under and stitching. Tuck the raw edge of one of your pieces of ribbon into the very top of one of the front centre seams. Stitch the front edge closed, remembering to continue around the bottom corner to close up the 2cm of the bottom hem left unstitched. Repeat on the other side.

Simply fasten the ribbon into a bow and the capelet is complete.

the
Owl

Owl Cape

Level:

Cutting and preparation:
30 mins

Sewing and finishing:
2-3 hrs

You will need:
- Pattern pieces M1–M7, B12–B15, I6 & I7
- Standard machine needles
- Matching machine threads
- 1 or 2 large buttons or toggles

Fabric (all measurements are based on largest size):
- 1.1m width x 2m length outer main fabric
- 1.5m width x 1.5m length lining fabric

Budding magicians, birds, bats or super heroes – the cape symbolises a child's world of magic and mystery. Our owl is rich and dramatic, and the velvet outer layer is a perfect warm and practical choice for summer parties or festivals.

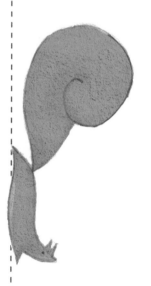

Finished garment size guide
Collar to bottom hem length:

1–2 years	41cm
2–3 years	44cm
3–4 years	47.5cm
4–5 years	51cm

FABRIC: This cape is made with cotton velvet as the outer fabric, lined with a lightweight cotton poplin. The velvet gives the cape extra thickness and warmth so that it can be used as a proper practical item. Velvet has a wonderful drape and adds a touch of extra magic in the way that it reflects light.

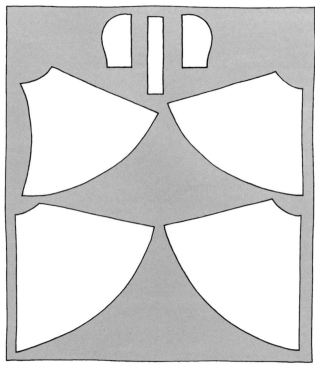

Instructions

1. Trace your pattern pieces, making note of any specific markings or instructions. Lay out the pattern pieces on your fabric and cut.

2. Start with the hood. Match your four ear pieces (M1) into pairs, right sides facing, and stitch along two of the edges, leaving the bottom open. Trim the excess seam around the top point, then turn and push out the corners with a chopstick/pencil.

3. Lay one of your hood outer back panels (I6) right side up, position the corresponding finished ear piece approximately 1cm from the top with the raw bottom edge of the ear lying along the straight front edge of the hood piece. Place the hood outer front panel (I7) on top of this, right side down, to sandwich the ear in between. Pin along the long straight edge and stitch, ensuring that you catch all of the layers. Repeat for the other side. Pin your hood outer central panel (B12), right sides facing, along the top curved edge of the outer hood section. Stitch from the top front

of the hood all the way down to the bottom. Pin the other side of the strip as you did for the other side of the hood so that the strip joins the two sides of the hood together.

4   Lay your hood inner central panel (B13) along the curved edge of the hood inner back panel (B14) and as with the outer pieces, pin and stitch. Repeat for the other side so that the centre strip joins the two sides of the hood together. Take your hood inner front panels (B15 – main fabric) and stitch together, right sides facing, along the top short straight edge. Open out and lay the long straight edge, right sides facing, along the entire front edge of the hood lining. Pin and stitch. Place the hood lining into the hood outer, right sides facing, aligning the front edges, and stitch. Turn right sides out, press around the front edge of the hood and top stitch this front edge.

5   Take your outer back pieces (M2) and attach down the centre back (shorter straight edge) with right sides facing. Next attach the longer side of each of your outer front pieces (M3 & M4) to the corresponding side edges of the attached outer back pieces, right sides facing. Repeat with your lining (M5, M6 & M7).

6   Pin your hood to the neckline of the cape outer with outer fabrics facing, aligning the centre point of the hood with the central seam at the back of the cape. Note that the front will be asymmetrical to allow for the overlap on one side. Attach, taking care to catch all of the layers.

7   Pin your lining, right sides facing, to the neck line of the outer body section, taking care to align at the centre back and shoulder seams. Stitch around the neck in order to sandwich your hood in between these layers, continue stitching around the curved button flap and don't stop until you've reached halfway down the front edge of the cape.

8   Align the bottom edge of the outer body with the bottom edge of the cape lining, right sides facing, pin at the seams and then continue to pin thoroughly in between. Stitch 0.5cm in around the entire bottom edge of the cape.

9   Pick up where you previously stitched halfway down the front central seam, leaving a substantial gap for turning, then start to stitch again. When you reach the bottom, the outer fabric will pull around by 0.5cm towards the lining side, continue to stitch through this overlap whilst pulling the seam allowance downwards, if possible, so that it will sit inside the hem. Next, take the central front edge on the opposite side and stitch closed. Trim the seam allowance around the curved buttonhole flap and at the other top corner.

10 Reach inside the gap and turn the cape right side out. Push out your corners using a chopstick/pencil. Press and pin the bottom hem, pulling it 0.5cm around to the lining side. Then press the front central hems, taking care to align the fabrics across your turning gap and allowing adequate seam allowance. Top stitch from the front edge of the hood around the buttonhole curve, down the front of the cape, across the entire bottom of the garment and returning up the other side, stopping at the opposite front hood point.

11 Have fun choosing a button or toggle or two to feature. Attach your buttonhole machine foot and amend the machine settings accordingly. Stitch your first buttonhole 0.5–1cm in from the edges on the side with the curved buttonhole flap. If you're using two buttons, position your second buttonhole 0.5–1cm in from the first. Carefully take your seam ripper and open up your buttonhole(s) – a pin placed across one end of the buttonhole creates the perfect barrier to prevent accidentally ripping out the other side. Mark with chalk where you'd like your button to sit on the other side, remembering that you are working with an asymmetrical overlap. Attach your button (see page 10).

Remember, as tempting as it may be, this cape is not intended for you. Do NOT don the cape!

Party Dress

It's party time and we've got it covered! With its bold tones and winged sleeves this owl dress really comes alive. Little ladies will feel elegant as they spin and twirl.

Level:

Cutting and preparation:
30 mins

Sewing and finishing:
1–2 hrs

You will need:
- Pattern pieces N1–N8
- 1 or 2 small buttons
- Matching threads
- Standard machine needles

Fabric (all measurements are based on largest size):
- 1.6m x 1.6m lightweight fabric, such as cotton poplin
- 1.6m width x 30cm length accent fabric for sleeve and skirt layering (one, two or three fabrics)

Please note that the skirt trim pieces are very wide and you may wish to cut these pieces separately rather than on the fold and just join at the short edges before attaching to the dress.

Finished garment size guide
Collar to bottom hem length:

12–18 months	45cm
18–24 months	49cm
2–3 years	53cm
3–4 years	57cm
4–5 years	61cm

Chest circumference:

12–18 months	58cm
18–24 months	60cm
2–3 years	62cm
3–4 years	64cm
4–5 years	66cm

FABRIC: This is a party dress, so anything goes. We've gone for a combination of lightweight cotton poplin fabrics in bold colours. It's a great excuse to go wild and really play around with colour. You could even get extra playful and use a different print for the bodice section; be brave, he who dares, wins!

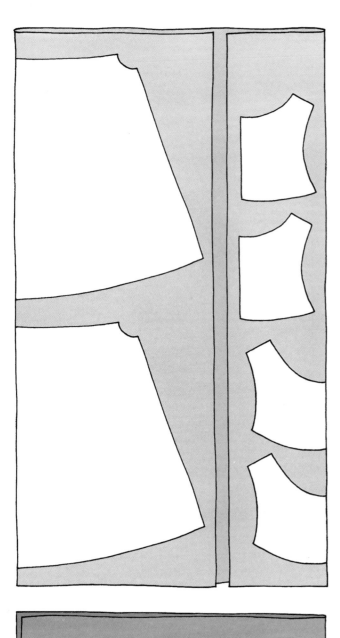

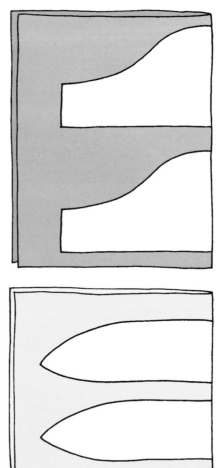

Instructions

1 Trace your pattern pieces, making note of any specific markings or instructions. Lay out the pattern pieces on your fabric and cut.

2 Start with the bodice. Take your outer bodice front (N1) and back (N2) pieces and attach at the shoulders. Repeat with the lining.

3 Lay your now-attached outer body pieces and lining pieces together, right sides facing, and pin. Stitch together from the bottom inner edge of the back pieces up the back, around the neckline (ensuring shoulder seams align), and then back down the other inner edge of the back piece.

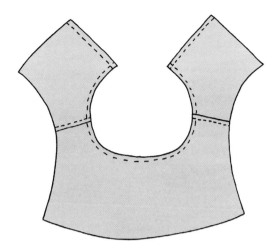

4 Turn the bodice right side out, push out the corners with a chopstick/pencil and press.

5 Decide how many buttons you would like to feature on the back, one button is probably enough. Measure out and mark with chalk where you'd like the centre of your button(s) to sit, then transfer any markings to the other side, allowing a 2.5cm centre cross-over on the pattern. Attach your sewing machine buttonhole foot and amend the machine settings accordingly. Place the fabric of the back central seam so that the start of the stitch will be around 0.5cm in from the finished edge, then go ahead and stitch your buttonhole. Repeat for any other buttonholes.

6 Carefully take your seam ripper and open up your buttonhole(s). (Remember the top tip of putting a pin at one end of the buttonhole to avoid ripping out the other side.)

7 Attach your button(s) on the other side of the bodice (see page 10). Button up your bodice pieces and at the bottom, where there is no button, use a pin to hold the 2.5cm overlap firmly in place.

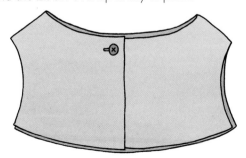

8 Take one of your thin skirt trim pieces (N3) and along the longest edge press 0.5cm and then 0.5cm to the wrong side and stitch. Repeat with the other thin skirt trim piece and for both wide skirt trim pieces (N4).

9 Take one of each of your now-hemmed skirt trim pieces and lay them right sides face up with the thin trim on top (right side of wide trim piece against wrong side of thin trim piece) with the long raw edges aligned. Join these trims with a basting stitch across the entire length of the top raw edge and gather (see page 10) to the width of the bottom edge of one of your skirt pieces (N5). Repeat with the other wide and thin skirt trim pieces.

10 Pin your trims, right sides facing, with raw edges aligned across the bottom length of each of the skirt pieces and attach. Press and top stitch the seam onto the main body of the skirt.

11 Take your front and back skirt pieces, run a basting stitch along the top raw edges and gather to the width of the bodice pieces (see page 10)– leave 3–5cm ungathered at each side of the body to centralise the gathering.

12 Pin the top gathered edge of one of your skirt pieces to the bottom curved raw edge of your front bodice section, right sides facing, and attach. Repeat with your other skirt piece, fastening it onto the back of your bodice, but take care to retain your 2.5cm overlap.

The Fox, the Bear & the Bunny

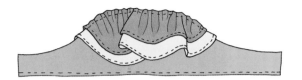

13 Next begin work on the sleeves. Take all of your six sleeve pieces (N6–N8), press 0.5cm and another 0.5cm to the wrong side along the bottom edges and top stitch to create a very small hem. Note: the middle and outer sleeve shapes are almost symmetrical but the bottom hem edge has a shallower curve, so make sure that you are pressing the correct edge.

14 Pin one of your outer sleeve pieces (N6) centrally on top of a middle sleeve piece (N7) with right sides of both pieces facing upwards. Set your machine stitch to its maximum length to create a basting stitch for gathering. Attach these two sleeve pieces using a basting stitch across the top raw edge and gather to a total width of 18cm, leaving 2cm ungathered at each end. Repeat with your other middle and outer sleeve pieces.

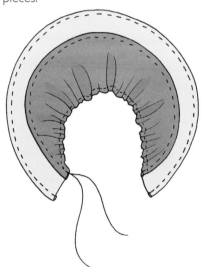

16 Pin your gorgeous little winged sleeves into place on your bodice armholes, aligning the centre point of your sleeves with the shoulder seams. The inner sleeve should run the entire length of the armhole. Stitch to attach, taking care to attach all the layers.

17 Fold one of your sleeves in half, right sides facing and stitch from the hemmed edge of the sleeve right down the side of the entire dress to the bottom hem. Return to the cuff hem area and stitch the end of the seam allowance flat to one side to both reinforce and avoid irritation, then do the same for the bottom hem. Repeat this whole process on the other side.

Dress made, time to get party planning!

15 Find the centre point of each of your sleeves' gathered edge and pin to the curved raw edge of your inner sleeve pieces, with right sides of both pieces facing upwards and lining up the central points. Continue to pin out from the centre along this raw edge and fasten with a standard stitch. It's a little fiddly but just take your time and it'll so be worth it!

the Bear

Paw Print Trousers

Level:

Cutting and preparation:
15 mins

Sewing and finishing:
1 hr

You will need:
- Pattern pieces O1 & O2
- Paw print appliqué (knee or bottom patch) can be found on page 123
- Standard machine needles
- 18mm-wide elastic
- Matching threads

Fabric (all measurements are based on largest size):
- 1.2m width x 75cm length medium-weight fabric
- Small piece of leatherette for appliqué patches

A little pair of pull-on trousers makes the perfect beginner's project, quick and simple to make.
The paw print appliqué helps personalise your work whilst injecting that all-important cute factor.

Finished garment size guide
Outer leg length:

12–18 months	47.75cm
18–24 months	51.5cm
2–3 years	55.25cm
3–4 years	59.5cm
4–5 years	64cm

Waist circumference (elastic measurement):

12–18 months	42cm
18–24 months	44cm
2–3 years	46cm
3–4 years	48cm
4–5 years	50cm

FABRIC: The paw print patches are made from leatherette and appliquéd onto a fine cotton corduroy. Although you could use almost any dressmaking fabric for these trousers, corduroy is great to work with as it is robust yet soft and behaves itself while being stitched! It also looks amazing in bright, bold colours that you can pair with almost anything. Leatherette is the perfect choice for appliqué as it does not fray, it can be cut into very neat shapes and it is hardwearing (which is important for patches on the knee or bottom!). You could also use felt or, if you're careful about fraying, printed cottons can make adorable appliqué patches.

A note on cutting appliqué shapes: The appliqué shapes for this project can be found on page 123. If you're using leatherette it is easiest to draw the pattern shape onto the back of the fabric and then cut to get a really neat shape. This should work well for most fabrics, especially with small pieces.

Instructions

1 Trace your pattern pieces, making note of any specific markings or instructions. Don't forget to trace and cut your little paw print for the knee or bottom (see page 123). Lay out the pattern pieces on your fabric and cut.

2 If you are choosing to do the knee appliqué, do this first. Take the front trouser piece (O1) that you'd like to appliqué (left or right) and use a chalk pencil to mark out the point where you'd like your paw print to sit, taking into consideration the 3cm top and 3cm bottom hem allowance. Don't use pins with the leatherette because it leaves holes, just hold the pieces in place as you sew. If you find this really fiddly, use some spray-on fabric adhesive. Start with your large paw piece and use an appliqué stitch to secure in place (see page 10). Position and attach your three small pieces by eye.

3 Take your two front pieces (O1), right sides facing, and attach from the top down the front centre seam to the crotch. Repeat for the back pieces (O2).

4 If you are doing the bottom appliqué, now is the time. Taking the now-attached back section of your trousers, mark out where you'd like your paw to sit, bearing in mind the 3cm top hem and seam allowance for the crotch. Go ahead and attach as described in step 2.

5 Attach your front pieces to your back pieces, right sides facing, along the outer leg side seams. Stitch the inner legs from the bottom of one leg, around the crotch and down the other leg, aligning the centre seams. It's a good idea to reinforce the crotch area for added durability.

7 Press your ankle hems 1cm and then 2cm to the wrong side. Turn the trousers right side out and finish your hems.

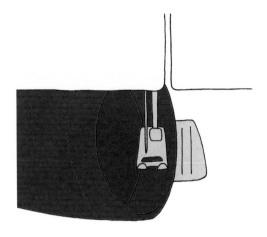

Quick, easy and irresistibly cute!

6 With the trousers still inside out, press 1cm and then another 2cm at the waist to the wrong side to make your elastic cavity. Cut your required amount of elastic (see size guide) and use a zigzag stitch to connect the two ends of your elastic with a small overlap, creating a loop of elastic. Insert the loop into the waist cavity. Close the cavity by stitching close to the folded edge, taking care to not catch the elastic. Pull the elastic through as you stitch to spread the gathering and allow the hem to sit flat.

Little Brown Bear Sweater

Level:

Cutting and preparation:
20 mins

Sewing and finishing:
1 hr

You will need:
- Pattern pieces P1–P6
- Jersey machine needles
- Matching threads

Fabric (all measurements are based on largest size):
- 1m width x 80cm length main fabric (stretch jersey)
- 60cm width x 40cm length stretch cuffing fabric

FABRIC: This sweater pattern has been designed with a stretchy fabric in mind; the gorgeous soft brown stretchy velour used here is reminiscent of cuddly teddy bears, and the cuffs are made from a stretchy dark brown ribbed fabric. You can play around with lighter- and heavier-weight jersey stretch fabrics depending on what sort of top you'd like to create.

With its simple shape and fuss free nature, this nostalgic little sweater is ultra-versatile and completely timeless. Plus, it's easily transformed with a bolder print or contrasting cuff. Check out our cat outfits (pages 32–38) for another colour popping approach.

Before you begin:
- Failing to use the fabric-appropriate needles may result in the fabric laddering at the seams, so do use jersey needles.
- As with all our patterns, a 0.75cm seam allowance has been included here. If using an overlocker machine there is no need to trim off any excess as the distance between the needles and blade of the machine should be approximately 0.75cm.
- Pin plenty – stretch fabrics like to move around!
- When feeding the fabric through the machine, take care not to pull or stretch it, as this would disfigure your garment and cause the pattern pieces to become unaligned. Let the machine do the work.
- Jersey fabric won't fray so there's no need to finish the raw edges on a sewing machine.

Finished garment size guide
Collar to bottom hem length:
12–18 months	31.25cm
18–24 months	33.25cm
2–3 years	35.25cm
3–4 years	37.75cm
4–5 years	39.75cm

Chest circumference:
12–18 months	56cm
18–24 months	58cm
2–3 years	60cm
3–4 years	62cm
4–5 years	64cm

The Fox, the Bear & the Bunny

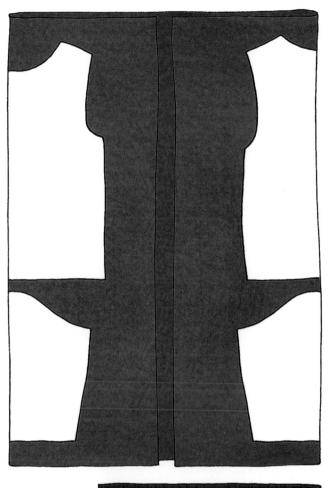

Instructions

1 Trace your pattern pieces, making note of any specific markings or instructions. Lay out the pattern pieces on your fabric and cut.

2 Set your sewing machine to a stretch stitch or set up your overlocker, if you have one.

3 Lay out the body front and back pieces (P1 & P2), right sides facing, and stitch together along both shoulder edges.

4 Take your neck cuffing piece (P3) and stitch together the two short edges, right sides facing, to create a continuous loop of fabric. Fold this loop in half lengthways with wrong sides facing and press to create the neck piece.

5 Open out the front and back of the sweater and lay it flat, right side up. Pin the neck loop into the neck hole with raw edges aligned and the seam of the neck loop pinned at one of the shoulder seams. Attach, taking extra care not to stretch the fabric as you stitch or you will end up with an ugly loose neckhole. Press the seam flat inwardly.

6 Take one of your sleeve upper pieces (P4) and pin the curved edge of the sleeve into the curve of the armhole, right sides facing. Make sure the centre of the sleeve curve sits at the shoulder seam. Stitch together and then repeat with your second sleeve.

7 Take one of your now-attached sleeves and fold it in half, right sides facing. Align the raw edge all the way from the end of the upper sleeve right down the entire side of the garment to the bottom edge and stitch together. Take it slowly as you stitch around the armpit curve as this is a real danger zone for not properly catching both pieces of fabric, which results in nasty holes. Repeat on the other side.

8 Take your two sleeve cuffs (P5) and fold each of them in half lengthways so that the slightly longer edges meet; stitch these together for each sleeve. Fold each cuff in half again, wrong sides facing, so that the remaining raw edges align, and press to create two little cuffs ready to be attached to your sweater.

9 Turn your main sweater body right side out and pin each of the sleeve cuffs around the raw edge of the upper sleeve, right sides facing. Stitch around to attach.

10 Finally, take your waistband cuffing piece (P6) and stitch together the two shortest edges, right sides facing, to create a continuous loop of fabric. Fold in half, wrong sides together, and press. Pin the waistband around the entire bottom edge of the body, right sides facing, aligning the seam of the waistband with one of the side seams of the body and attach.

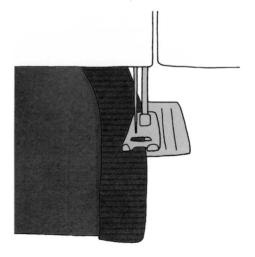

This little sweater is so
adorably retro and it's so easy
to vary the fabric weight to
suit any season.

Bear Duffle Coat

Level:

Cutting and preparation:
1-2 hrs

Sewing and finishing:
8-10 hrs

You will need:
- Pattern pieces B3, B5–B8, B12–B19,I2, I6–I8, Q1–Q4
- 4 toggles
- 2 large sleeve buttons
- 1m cording
- Matching machine threads
- Standard machine needles
- Snap popper fastener tool
- 4 sets of snap popper fastener inserts

Fabric (all measurements are based on largest size):
- 1.5m width x 1.5m length outer main fabric
- 1.5m width x 1.1m length lining fabric
- 1m width x 50cm length outer accent fabric
- 50cm width x 50cm length leatherette

This bear coat is a subtle and stylish adaptation of a traditional duffle. With his broad furry chest and fluffy ears he offers a fabulous sprinkling of personality in a child's coat.

Before you begin:
This is a big project. There are a lot of pattern pieces and fabric, so it's important to be super organised, perhaps set out the pieces according to the coat sections – place all the hood pieces in a pile, all the lining bits, sleeves, etc. Or, if you prefer, just sort them according to their fabric type. It's also a good idea to keep the pattern pieces with their corresponding fabric pieces so that when they are mentioned by reference number, you know which piece to grab.

A note on cutting fur and leatherette:
For the leatherette it is easiest to draw the pattern shape onto the back of the leatherette multiple times and then cut to get a really consistent shape. For the fur, place the pattern on the wrong side of the fabric and cut it that way rather than trying to get a clean cut line amongst a deep pile of fur.

FABRIC: The outer fabric here is a synthetic coat-grade felt, lined with cotton poplin. The accent fabric is a luxury deep-pile brown fur and black leatherette is used for finishing touches. Using synthetic felt adds a touch more complexity to the project because you cannot press the fabric (it will melt!). If you use a synthetic felt then instead of pressing you will need to top stitch all of the seams and include lots of extra pinning at each stage. It looks lovely and gives a very professional-looking finish, but it does take more time.

Finished garment size guide
Collar to bottom hem length:

1–2 years	37.25cm
2–3 years	40.5cm
3–4 years	43.75cm
4–5 years	47cm

Chest circumference:

1–2 years	68cm
2–3 years	70cm
3–4 years	72cm
4–5 years	74cm

Instructions

1 Trace your pattern pieces, making note of any specific markings or instructions. Sort your pattern pieces into piles according to fabric type, then lay out pieces on your fabric and cut.

2 Begin with the outer body pieces. Pin the bottom edge of one of your outer front upper panels (Q1) to the corresponding (short) edge on one of the outer front lower panels (Q2) and attach. Top stitch the seam allowance onto the lower front body piece approximately 0.5cm from the seam. Repeat with the other side. Take your outer front centre panels (B3) and attach each one to the front centre raw edge of

the main body pieces. Top stitch the seam allowance towards the front centre panels.

3 Stitch together your front and outer back (B5) pieces at the shoulders.

4 Take your four cuff pieces (I2) and pair them, right sides facing. Stitch around the edge leaving just the shortest straight edge open. Trim the seam allowance around the curve. Take a chopstick and use it to carefully turn the cuff pieces right side out. Press flat.

5 Place your pressed cuff pieces with the short raw edge at the side of each outer sleeve (B19) approximately 7cm from the bottom edge of the sleeve. Make sure that with the arms lying side by side you have created a mirror image resulting in a left and a right sleeve. Pin securely in place and top stitch to attach. Position your two large buttons in the centre of the curved end of the cuff strap and attach.

6 Align the curved edge of each outer sleeve with the curve of the armholes on your outer body piece, right sides facing; pin together, ensuring that the centre of the sleeve lines up with the shoulder seam and stitch to attach. Make sure that you are affixing the correct sleeve to the correct armhole; the button on the cuff strap should sit towards the back of the body.

7 Fold each sleeve in half lengthways, right sides facing, and stitch along the raw edges continuing down the side of the body, ensuring that the underarm seams align – this is a real danger zone for not properly catching both pieces of fabric. If you are going to reinforce anywhere, do it now.

8 Lay each of your pocket lining pieces (B7 – lining fabric) onto the pocket outer pieces (B7 – main fabric), right sides facing, and stitch, leaving just the top straight edge open. Trim the excess seam allowance around the curved corners and turn right side out. Repeat the same process with each of the two pocket flaps (B8). Press all of the pocket pieces, taking care to

pull the fabric slightly towards the lining side, creating a very small border of your outer fabric on the inner side (this will prevent your lining from peeping around the edge when top stitching later). Press a 1cm seam inwardly to the wrong side of the fabrics along the top edge of your two main pocket pieces. Stitch across this top edge. Take your pocket flaps and finish the raw edge of both fabrics together with a zigzag or edging stitch, then press 0.75cm to the lining side across this top edge.

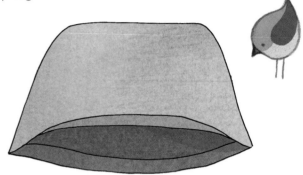

9 With your coat outer body laid right side up, position and pin your two main pockets in place, measuring approximately 7cm up from the bottom straight edge and 11cm in from the front centre raw edge. Top stitch around each pocket and then return to each of the top corners and run a few stitches diagonally across each side for added strength. Pin your two pocket flaps in place with the folded finished edge 0.75cm up from the top of the main pocket, allow it to close over and top stitch across the top straight edge.

10 The next job is to make the hood. Grab all of your hood and ear pieces and start by making the ears. Take one of your outer ear pieces (Q3) and your inner ear accent fabric piece (Q4) and use an appliqué zigzag stitch (see page 10) to attach, centrally aligned at the bottom edge. Repeat for the other ear. Lay both of your remaining two outer ear pieces flat and place each of your appliquéd ear fronts on top, right sides facing. Stitch around, leaving just the bottom straight edge open. Turn your ears right side out, using a

chopstick or the wrong side of a pencil to push out the seams. Press on the non-appliquéd side.

11 Now make the main part of the hood. With your hood outer back panel (I6) laid right side up, position one of your finished ear pieces, appliquéd side up, approximately 2cm from the top with the straight bottom edge of the ear lying along the straight front edge of the hood piece. Place the hood outer front panel (I7) on top of this, right side down, sandwiching the ear between the front and back panels. Pin along the long straight edge and stitch, ensuring that you catch all of the layers. Repeat for the other side with your corresponding hood and ear pieces. With right sides facing, pin the long straight edge of the hood outer central panel (B12) along the curved edge of the outer hood section and stitch from the top front of the hood all the way down to the bottom. Pin the other side of the central panel as you did for the other side of the hood so that the strip joins the two sides of the hood together.

12 For the hood lining, lay your hood inner central strip (B13) along the curved edge of one of the hood inner back panels (B14) and as with the outer pieces, pin and stitch. Repeat for the other side so that the centre strip joins the two sides of the hood together. Take your hood inner front panels (B15 – main fabric) and stitch together, right sides facing, along the top short straight edge. Open out and lay the long straight edge, right sides facing, along the entire front edge of the hood lining pieces. Pin and stitch. Place the hood lining into the hood outer, right sides facing, aligning the front edges and stitch. Turn right sides out, press around the front edge of the hood and top stitch this front edge.

13 Now attach the hood to the coat outer body. Find the central point of the base of the hood and pin, outer sides facing, to the back centre of the neckline of the coat. Continue to pin around securely and attach.

14 Once the lining is complete you can bring all the components together into one adorable (and super stylish) bear coat! Place one of your front inner side panels (B16), right sides facing, against your corresponding front inner middle panel (B17 – main fabric). Pin together along the long curved edge and stitch. Repeat for the other side. Attach the shoulder (top short edge) of each of these to the corresponding shoulder of the inner back piece (B18). Open out your now-attached lining and pin the top curve of the sleeve lining (B6) into the armhole curve, ensuring that the centre of the sleeve sits at the shoulder seam. Attach and repeat for the other side.

15 Fold each lining sleeve in half lengthways, right sides facing, and stitch along the raw edges, continuing down the side of the body, ensuring that the underarm seams align. As with the outer pieces, you can reinforce this stitch just around the underarm area to strengthen the seams.

16 If you are going to feature popper fasteners in your coat, now is the time to insert them. Lay out your coat outer and use a chalk pencil to mark the positioning for your poppers on the front centre panel of the child's left side (right side to look at). Sit the first popper fairly close to the top to provide a nice snug seal against the cold, remembering to leave seam allowance. Place three more poppers at regular

intervals down the coat, taking the last popper no lower than the mid-point of the pocket; remember to leave space for a hem plus the leatherette triangles. The poppers for the other side of the coat will go on the lining piece: so be sure to align the top edges of the lining and outer body pieces to transfer your markings across to the child's right side of the lining piece. There is 4cm difference in length between the lining and outer pieces so it is important that your poppers line up from the top edge and not the bottom. Now insert your popper fasteners, but first check and check again that you have correctly aligned your poppers.

17 Pin your lining, right sides facing, to the neckline of the outer body section, taking care to align at the shoulder seams. Stitch around the neck opening in order to sandwich your hood in between these layers. This is probably the trickiest part of this project, just pin plenty, take it slow and you will manage just fine.

18 Sometimes you can be left with a bit of a wonky line running across the entire bottom width of your outer and lining body pieces where all the different pieces have joined. If this is the case, take your scissors and tidy it up but note that the lining is intended to be 4cm shorter than the outer body section so don't chop this off! Take measurements to compare each side in length so that you aren't left with one side of the coat hanging slightly lower than the other. Now that you have a lovely straight line to work with, pin together the outer and lining body pieces, right sides facing, along the bottom raw edge and stitch 2cm in from the edge.

19 Take one side of your coat and stitch the front central edge closed, starting from the top. When you reach the bottom, the outer coat will pull around by 2cm towards the lining side; continue to stitch through this overlap whilst pulling the seam allowance downwards so it will sit inside the hem. Take the other side and instead of closing this up entirely, you'll need to leave a large gap for pulling the entire coat right side out.

Begin stitching from the top, then part way down leave your gap and resume stitching, ensuring that you are left with the same 2cm overlap at the bottom as before. You can carefully trim the two top corners to remove any bulk from the collar.

20 Reach inside the gap that you have left and begin to turn your garment. Take your chopstick/pencil and push out all the corners. Press your coat starting at the front seams. On the side that you have left open, fold in the same seam allowance along the gap, retaining a consistent straight edge.

21 When pressing along the bottom hem, reach back inside the lining to make sure the 2cm seam allowance is pushed downwards to sit within the hem and pin this in place. Top stitch a 1cm hem across the entire bottom of the coat and then top stitch the two front edges, closing your turning gap as you go.

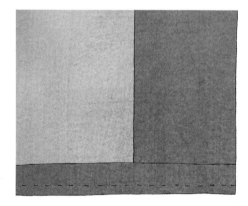

22 Push your outer body sleeve through the sleeve lining so that your sleeve is inside out. Press 1cm of the outer sleeve towards the wrong side and another 2cm towards the wrong side to make your sleeve hem. The edge of the lining should sit fully inside this hem. Repeat on the other side. Turn sleeves right side out and top stitch the hem.

23 Cut eight 12cm lengths of cording and insert four of them through your chosen toggles. Place to one side. Lay out your coat and pin or mark with chalk where you'd like your toggles to be – arranging them between the poppers gives a good seal down the front of the coat. Affix your toggles to the coat with a small reinforced stitch on the child's left side. Attach your remaining loops of cording to the opposite side making sure they line up with the toggles.

24 Finally, take your 8 leatherette triangles (I8) and use a standard straight stitch to top stitch them over the raw ends of the cording – you can disguise the under-stitching by using a coordinating thread on top and keeping the bobbin the same colour as the main body of the coat.

And there you have it, the perfect coat for a trip to the woods.

Appliqué Templates

Fox-face Dungarees (page 54)
Appliqué Template.

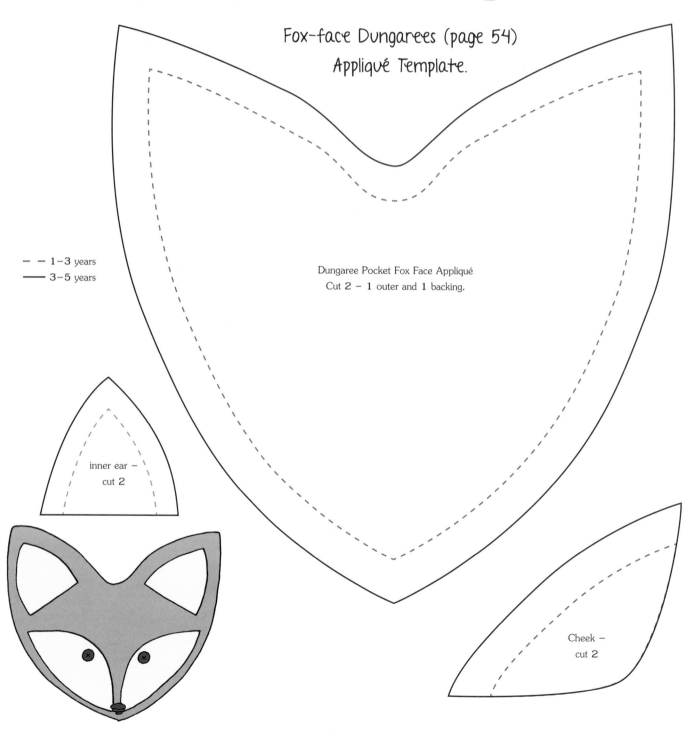

1 – 3 years
3 – 5 years

Dungaree Pocket Fox Face Appliqué
Cut 2 – 1 outer and 1 backing.

inner ear –
cut 2

Cheek –
cut 2

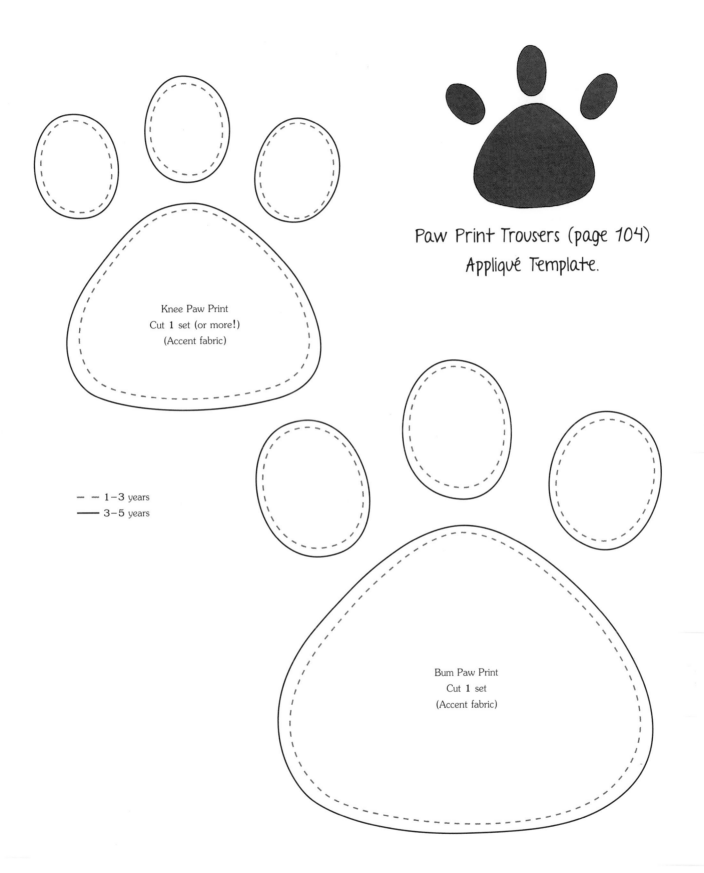

Knee Paw Print
Cut **1** set (or more!)
(Accent fabric)

Paw Print Trousers (page 104)
Appliqué Template.

— — 1–3 years
—— 3–5 years

Bum Paw Print
Cut **1** set
(Accent fabric)

Paw Print Mittens (page 42)
Applique Template

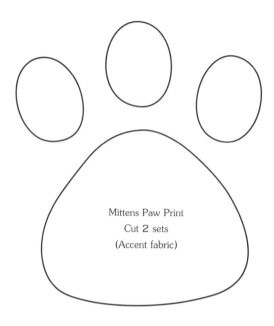

Mittens Paw Print
Cut 2 sets
(Accent fabric)

Mouse Pocket Pinafore Dress (page 76)
Appliqué Template.

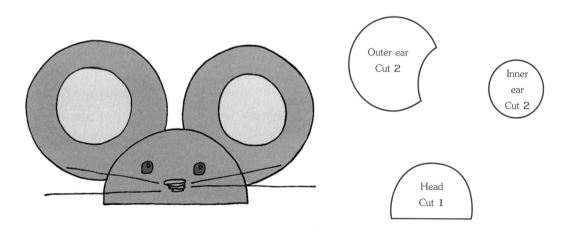

Outer ear
Cut 2

Inner
ear
Cut 2

Head
Cut 1

Suppliers & Resources

There are online fabric stores popping up all the time and we urge you to shop around. Trusty old Ebay is great and we still use it for the odd bit of kit, haberdashery and indeed fabric. It's easy to fall into habits of returning to the same old places, we have to remind ourselves to use our search engines differently and seek out those little gems, lovely new suppliers and original fabrics that inspire new ideas. We predominantly source within the UK; the fabric isn't cheap but the postage is and it fulfils our impatient nature to receive our supplies within a day or so. Below are a few of our favourite outlets.

Dragonfly Fabrics

Dragonfly Fabrics have a strong focus on quality. They offer some gorgeous cotton jersey knits, which is our all-time favourite fabric type for children's clothing.
www.dragonflyfabrics.co.uk
Dragonfly Fabrics
Mayfield
East Sussex, TN20 6TX
Email: sales@dragonflyfabrics.co.uk

Fabric Rehab

Fabric addict? Then this store will definitely appeal. In terms of high quality cotton poplin, what you can't find at Fabric Rehab just isn't worth having! We love the fact that they organise their store both by fabric type and fabric theme: it makes browsing so much easier.
www.fabricrehab.co.uk
Fabric Rehab
3B Dedham Vale Business Centre
Manningtree Road, Dedham
Essex, CO7 6BL.
Telephone: 01206 321611

Organic Textile Company

We found this company when we were searching for soft, child-friendly denim, and also enjoy working with their natural undyed range. Not only do they have the most wonderful business ethos, you're likely to find something really original.
www.organiccotton.biz/store
Organic Textile Company
43–45 Maengwyn St
Machynlleth
Powys, SY20 8EB
Email: phil@organiccotton.biz

Plush Addict

Plush Addict have an incredible variety of dressmaking fabrics including some of our favourite fabric designers such as Michael Miller and Robert Kaufman, who produce bright, fun and stylish fabrics that are ideal for making children's clothing.
www.plushaddict.co.uk
78–80 Papyrus Road
Peterborough, PE4 5BH
Telephone 1 : 0800 048 8787 (UK Free Phone)
Telephone 2: +44 1733 808950 (from outside UK)
Email : sales@plushaddict.co.uk